THE I-FILES

True Reports of Unexplained Phenomena in Illinois

jay rath

**With a foreword by Anne Bell,
research scientist at NASA's Ames Research Center**

Trails Books
Madison, Wisconsin

Library of Congress Catalog Card Number: 99-72897
ISBN: 0-915024-74-8

Editor: Stan Stoga
Cover Designer: Kate Orenberg
Illustrations: Jay Rath

Printed in the United States of America.

06 05 04 03 02 01 00 99   6 5 4 3 2 1

This book was not approved, prepared, licensed,
or endorsed by any entity involved in creating or producing *The X-Files*.

Trails Media Group, Inc.
P.O. Box 5650 • Madison, WI 53705
(800) 236-8088 • e-mail: info@wistrails.com
www.wistrails.com

For Christy

CONTENTS

ACKNOWLEDGMENTS

I would like to thank Loren Coleman for his assistance, and *FATE* magazine; my thanks also to Dr. Gerald Olson of the University of Wisconsin. I especially thank Anne Bell. I also wish to express my gratitude to Kim Moucha, Vicki Coleman, Fred Olsen, and Angela Tate. Excerpts from *Messages From Our Heavenly Mother to Her Children* are used by permission of the author, Ray Doiron.

FOREWORD

When Jay first told me about his plans for a book documenting local experiences with unexplained phenomena, I asked him if there was going to be a "how-to" chapter. Not how to learn about unexplained phenomena, mind you, but how to actually encounter one yourself.

My tongue-in-cheek inquiry reveals one reason for the enduring popularity of these stories, especially firsthand accounts: they appeal to our desires to experience something truly beyond everyday existence. Even Carl Sagan, who argued for a rational and scientific approach to the universe and who compared the current wave of UFO sightings to earlier episodes of possession by spirits, made first contact with alien cultures the subject of his only novel, *Contact*.

It doesn't take much reflection to see the plot line of *Contact* as a fictional exercise in wish fulfillment. The realities of adulthood force almost all of us to abandon childhood dreams of being an astronaut going into outer space, but at least there's a chance that outer space might come to us.

Another reason that unexplained phenomena capture our imagination is that they are, well, unexplained. A world in which everything goes according to plan and every experience can be neatly analyzed by the rational part of our brains is just plain boring. A race of wild semi-humans descended from Neanderthals lurking in the northern woods, aliens both benign and ill intentioned that visit in the night to dispense pancakes or disembowel cattle, ancient cultures that disappear into the mists of time, and ancient creatures that lurk beneath the surface of otherwise placid lakes: these are food for the imagination, and Jay serves them up cooked just right.

His reports are well researched and engagingly presented, avoiding both the dry earnestness of the true believer and the sour contempt of the confirmed skeptic. Most important, they are seasoned with a healthy dose of humor.

Maybe in the end these accounts of unexplained phenomena are just vicarious thrills, but I'll take what I can get.

Anne Bell, research scientist
NASA's Ames Research Center*

---

* It was at Ames, in Mountain View, California, that the first identification was made of amino acids that originated elsewhere in the universe besides our planet. They were found in the debris of a meteor that had fallen to earth. Amino acids are the building blocks of molecular life.

INTRODUCTION

During the ensuing year there will be authenticated
sightings of roughly 200 Unidentified Flying Objects,
of which the Pentagon will be able to disprove 210.
—Life magazine, January 6, 1958[*]

'm in a park in a cold Wisconsin spring. In front of and behind me is
lake ice too thin for skaters anymore, and so we are alone on this island in the center of the park. I'm with a man I met some years ago,
and we walk nonstop as I try to take notes on my steno pad.

We'd just eaten lunch, but in restaurants are people, and people
sometimes listen, and so we are now in a park where we can see anyone
approaching from a long, long way off. My friend is telling me how to
find a former National Security Agency employee who can tell me of the
government's secret UFO studies. He is telling me about his own UFO
sighting aboard a U.S. Navy cruiser in the Atlantic. He is telling me about
his Navy missile and radar training. He is telling me about the crashed
flying saucer that was brought to Chicago's Great Lakes Naval Training
Center, and the specific building where it was—maybe is—hidden.

---

[*] I am indebted to the late journalist Frank Edwards for locating this observation.

The last time we'd spoken in person, years earlier, my unlisted phone number was somehow turned up by a man who called himself George, who claimed to have ties with various U.S. intelligence agencies. He called me and advised me that if I persisted, my phone would be tapped, my mail rerouted and opened, resealed and then sent on its way. Years later, while working on my first book on unexplained phenomena, George visited my home while I was away and spooked my housemates.

I have a great job.

This is a book that I hope can fit into many categories but most especially anthropology. I like to plot the advance of unexplained phenomena across the history of humanity. Today's UFO from Zeta Reticula was a 1950s flying saucer from Venus, and 2,000 years before that it was a sign from a God, no matter what the witnesses' religions. Bigfoot was the Native Americans' Windigo, the Ancient Greeks' Minotaur, and perhaps even the Bible's "giants in those days."

We have always embraced the unknown, but in recent decades we have tended to sneer at its entire continuum, with the mysteries of religion on the one end and alien conspiracies on the other. But with the current dose of millennium fever has come a cultural thawing. Never mind that the year 2000 is a date that has significance only to the Christians who began time with the year 1 A.D.; we have been starving ourselves of mystery, and we'll take it wherever we can find it. I like to think that this is healthy, and that it is a sign of critical thinking. Suddenly we are willing to be convinced of new ideas. We've too long accepted whatever we were told.

For most of us, as an example, electricity might as well be magic. We accept it without thinking about it—at least since we've grown up. You and I know what it does, but do we know what it *is*? For all I know, the computer I'm writing this with is filled with magic pixies who make the words appear on the screen. And if I opened it up and looked at all the circuit boards, I would have no evidence to the contrary. The little doodads inside are beyond my comprehension. In every way that counts, they are magic.

But flying saucers, or an animal that walks like a man—these are mysteries that I can get my fingers around and wonder about for myself. All the experts are self-appointed, and I have as good a chance at finding the truth as anyone. Astronomy, metallurgy, journalism, folklore—virtually any discipline is a background for it. And as Prof. Robert Brightman pointed out to me at the Anthropology Department of the University of Wisconsin, on the beginning of my journey into the unexplained, along the way I'll learn at least a little about humanity.

In determining the distinction between Bigfoot and people, for example, I create a tighter definition of what it means to be a person. If Bigfoot isn't a member of the humans-only club, then what rules does he violate? The answer says more about us than about any monster.

I've written books similar to this one on unexplained phenomena in Wisconsin and Minnesota, but I had no idea of the rich treasures waiting for me in Illinois: giant birds, lake monsters, at least one crop circle, one ghost ship and many more lost without reason, countless UFO sightings, and reports not only of Bigfoot but of kangaroos, and possibly even the Chupacbras. In Chicago was taken the first UFO photo ever, in 1897.

I hope the reader will excuse me when I introduce a little information from neighboring states, but of course these phenomena do not respect political boundaries, and they are best appreciated from a regional perspective. In the end, this is a uniquely Illinoisan book, and every place name is in Illinois unless otherwise stated or unless it is a major city. I like restricting my work to individual areas: it is easy to discount a UFO report from Bolivia, for example, for some stupid reason having to do with geographic bias. But a sighting in Chicago? "Well, there might be something to this."

I hope you will find humor, mystery, horror, and even science here. Thank you for taking the risk of being convinced.

An Invitation

If you have stories about unexplained phenomena from any state, please share them with me. I may be reached in care of Wisconsin Trails, P.O. Box 5650, Madison, WI 53703.

Partial Bibliography

The material for this book came from a variety of sources, including personal interviews, U.S. Air Force files, the National UFO Reporting Center, and newspapers. Other printed sources include:

Blum, Howard. *Out There.* New York: Simon and Schuster, 1990.

Bowen, Charles, ed. *The Humanoids.* Chicago: Henry Regnery Company, 1969.

Bryan, C.D.B. *Close Encounters of the Fourth Kind: Alien Abduction, UFOs, and the Conference at M.I.T.* New York: Alfred A. Knopf, 1995.

Byrne, Peter. *The Search for Bigfoot: Monster, Myth, or Man?* New York: Pocket Books, 1976.

Cohen, Daniel. *The Great Airship Mystery.* New York: Dodd, Mead & Co., 1981.

Coleman, Loren. *Mysterious America.* Boston: Faber and Faber, 1983.

Condon, Edward. *Scientific Study of Unidentified Flying Objects.* Washington, D.C.: U.S. Department of Commerce, 1968.

Corliss, William. *Handbook of Unusual Natural Phenomena.* Garden City, New York: Anchor Press/Doubleday, 1983.

Fawcett, Lawrence, and Barry J. Greenwood. *Clear Intent: The Government Coverup of the UFO Experience.* Englewood Cliffs, N.J.: Prentice-Hall, Inc., 1984.

Gourley, Jay. *The Great Lakes Triangle.* Greenwich, Conn.: Fawcett, 1977.

Green, Gabriel. *Let's Face the Facts about Flying Saucers.* New York: Popular Library, 1967.

Green, John. *The Sasquatch File.* Agassiz, British Columbia: Cheam Publishing Ltd., 1973.

Hall, Richard, ed. *The UFO Evidence.* Washington, D.C.: National Investigations Committee on Aerial Phenomena, 1964.

Hynek, J. Allen. *The Hynek UFO Report*. New York: Dell Publishing Co., Inc., 1977.

Leslie, Desmond, and George Adamski. *Flying Saucers Have Landed*. London: Werner Laurie, 1953.

Marrs, Jim. *Alien Agenda*. New York: HarperCollins Publishers, Inc., 1997.

Napier, John. *Bigfoot*. New York: Berkley Medallion Books, 1972.

Olsen, Thomas M. *The Reference for Outstanding UFO Reports*. Riderwood, Md.: UFO Information Retrieval Center, Inc., 1966.

Ruppelt, Edward J. *The Report on Unidentified Flying Objects*. Garden City, N.Y.: Doubleday & Company, 1956.

Shackley, Myra. *Still Living? Yeti, Sasquatch, and the Neanderthal Enigma*. New York: Thames and Hudson, 1983.

Vallee, Jacques. *Passport to Magonia: From Folklore to Flying Saucers*. Chicago: Henry Regnery Co., 1969.

CHAPTER 1
CHICAGO, CITY OF THE BIG...SAUCERS

On March 11, 1999, the crew of an airliner coming into Chicago were burned by a glowing green UFO. That's just one of the most recent stories.

Second City, the Windy City, the City That Works, the City with Broad Shoulders, the City That Was Burned Down by a Cow, might as well be called Saucer Central. And so it should be; as we'll find, it is likely that the government's studies of UFOs have long been centered here.

Chicago has an incredible number of documented UFO reports, more than 60, many of them outstanding. And no one remembers them. Since the 1890s, each visit has been seen as an isolated event, without anyone noticing that for some strange reason *they* were interested in vacationing on the southern shore of Lake Michigan. Perhaps they like to watch *Bozo*.

Some might even argue that the modern flying saucer was *invented* in Chicago.

Yes, you're as likely here as anywhere to see a UFO, meet an alien, or—worse. Some of the craft brazenly fly into downtown Chicago to abduct residents for bizarre experiments, or so says a man called Jim (not his real name), whom we'll meet again later. He's been taken by "visitors" countless times from his urban Chicago home.

"Chicago presents no problem for them," Jim has said. "When they are ready, they do as they please. Also, their apparently high understanding of physics allows for much of their ability to defy the laws of reality as we now understand them. The alien craft can be 'cloaked.' I think there are several ways of going about this from what I have gathered. One is that they can assume the appearance of a conventional aircraft. The tip-off is that they will hover in a conspicuous place, for example outside of a window."

So watch for those conventional aircraft hovering outside your window! And meanwhile, get out the sunscreen—or suffer the burns that airliner crew acquired on March 11.

It was about 9 p.m. The pilot and copilot had for some time been watching a display of what they thought were northern lights. They were descending for their landing and were astounded to see the lights of the aurora borealis "stretch above and over the aircraft." The colors reflected off the plane's surfaces. Then there was a short "pulse of green light," which appeared to be "concentrated in a green 'ball.'" It approached the aircraft from the north, apparently at a very rapid velocity.

As late-night talk-show host Art Bell and the National UFO Reporting Center would later announce, "Immediately following the event, all members of the cockpit crew began to experience a sensation on their faces, as if they had been 'burnt by the sun.' They reported this sensation to each other, at which point the crew immediately..." Well, you'll never guess. They did not land. They did not get the hell out of there. They did not ditch into Lake Michigan. They did not alert the passengers, telling them to prepare for the worst, or ask onboard tourists to take pictures. No, the flight crew "requested clearance to divert to a different altitude."

"After the aircraft passed through a thin layer of overcast," the report continued, "the sensation of burning that the crew members had experienced seemed to them to disappear immediately." The green light was gone. But the next morning, at least one crew member noticed that his or her skin was red and sore and arranged to see a doctor. The crew had had a close encounter of the second kind: interaction by a UFO with its environment.

Another UFO was reported nearby just a few nights later. At 7 a.m. on March 19, a Chicagoan was heading north on Route 53 when "I noticed an object in the sky heading west, moving fast. Having airports to the northeast [O'Hare] and east [Midway] and even a small airport to the west, air traffic is always present in this area. When the object quickly reversed direction heading east, I knew right away that this was no ordinary aircraft. As the object moved east it then changed direction, heading straight up, disappearing as it left my range of sight. I also noticed an airliner just to the east of the object approximately 20 miles distant. The object appeared to be a sphere and silver colored."

There are precedents for sightings from aircraft. In the 1950s it seemed downright popular for a while—popular for aliens, anyway—to buzz airliners. Such sightings now, however, are rare; it seems that UFOs have better things to do. Or more likely, such events are just not reported, thanks to the air force and the airline companies encouraging commercial pilots to keep quiet. (Military pilots even today can face fines and imprisonment for going public with sightings, though they are required to report the sightings in house—through the proper channels.)

On April 27, 1950, on its way to Chicago from South Bend Airport, a Trans-World airliner encountered a red, glowing saucer that flew alongside. It had overtaken the plane at about 2,000 feet. After calming the passengers, Captain Robert Adickes and First Officer Robert Manning—somewhat disturbingly—turned toward the craft. The saucer ducked beneath the plane. After a few minutes, the UFO sped away.

"I had just had my dinner and was wide awake," said Adickes. "It was definitely round, with no irregular features at all, and about 10 to 20 percent as thick as it was round. It was very smooth and streamlined, and glowed evenly with a bright red color as if it were heated stainless steel. It was so bright it gave off a light. It left no vapor, no flame. It appeared to fly on edge, like a wheel going down a highway." Passenger C. W. Anderson said it looked like a big red lightbulb, fading away quickly. Passenger Jacob Goelzer said it looked like "a spinning exhaust, all aflame."

These are just a few of the city's many UFO reports. UFOs were seen over Chicago on July 1, 1950; July 4, 1950; November 8, 1957; February 6, 1961; January 3, 1974; January 10, 1975; July 23, 1975; and

October 10, 1975. And these are just the reports for which I do not have narrative details.

Many of the sightings came at the dawn of the modern UFO age, in 1947. Long before then strange shapes and lights had been seen in the world's skies, but it wasn't until two years after the end of World War II, on June 24, 1947, that the public embraced the idea of alien visitors. On that day, pilot Kenneth Arnold told a widely publicized story of nine shiny, curved flying wings he had seen over the Cascade Mountains in Washington state. They had flown at an estimated 1,600 miles per hour, in a strange skipping motion, something like the way saucers might look if you skipped them across water. The name "flying saucers" caught, and soon they were seen by everyone everywhere.

The "news" publisher who made the most out of Arnold's sighting was Chicago's own Ray Palmer. He edited a number of pulps, sensational magazines printed on cheap paper. His *Amazing Stories* and *Fantastic Adventures* magazines were bestsellers. Even before Arnold's encounter, Palmer had laid the groundwork with stories of alien encounters, some clearly fictional and others offered as fact. One of Palmer's favorite theories was that the saucers came from a secret hollow-earth civilization ruled by the Detrimental Robots, which he abbreviated as "Deros." The Deros manipulated humanity with their projected thought rays. Palmer's source was a Pennsylvania welder who drew on "racial memory" for his accounts.

It is not generally known that Palmer had his own Chicago UFO sighting, a few years after he had turned his attentions almost exclusively to the phenomenon. There were apparently no Deros involved (my own theory is that they had by then turned their thought-projection rays toward Washington, D.C.). In fact, I find it very interesting that the sensational publisher's own account is, within the context of UFO reports, rather unremarkable. His description sounds identical to those of the small, fiery UFOs that Allied and Nazi pilots reported were trailing them in the waning days of World War II. Nicknamed "foo-fighters" by the Allies after a nonsense term in the popular "Smokey Stover" comic strip, they were thought to be a German secret weapon. To the Nazis they were just as much of a mystery, though there is some evidence that work on a German weapon resembling UFO descriptions had been carried out. The small fireballs were also observed in the war's Pacific Theater.

Palmer's sighting came on February 3, 1952, at 10 seconds past 6 p.m. He saw an orange globe emitting blue flashes, speeding past his home at an estimated 180 miles per hour. "It was approximately 15 feet off the ground and passed between a slope in the background and the trunks of large trees in the foreground," Palmer said. "The object was approximately the size of a basketball, and the light it emitted illuminated the ground beneath it and the slope behind it. The appearance of the globe was suggestive of the exhaust of a jet or rocket, although it left no trail behind it, nor did it seem elongated as might be expected of such a method of propulsion. If an object was being propelled by the orange, globular glow, it was not visible."

A man with an unusual sense of humor, Palmer devoted the rest of his life to circulating true accounts of sightings that even he sometimes had trouble believing. Before his death in 1977, he told UFO researcher Jim Moseley, "What if I told you it was all a joke?" But even if he didn't invent the "flying saucer," Palmer certainly invented the public's perception of it.

Others needed no convincing by Palmer. The same day as Palmer's sighting came the very first Chicago report. At 8:35 a.m. on June 25, 1947, Mrs. Nels Thor, of South Forest Avenue, observed a moon-size disk for 12 minutes as it hovered in the eastern sky over Lake Michigan. She said it glowed golden. It finally drifted into a cloud where, apparently, it disappeared.

At 2 a.m. the next morning, Mrs. J. M. Harrison, of Oakenwald Avenue, looked out her window and saw a huge ball of fire, five or six times larger than the moon. It moved to the northwest and then diminished in size. It then broke into many small disks that "whirled rapidly in a circle." She estimated that there were two or three dozen of the small disks, which moved so quickly that an accurate count was impossible.

Sightings continued. George Jones saw a UFO on July 6, as did Ida Bauer, Jean Dorsett, and George Wilkinson, each independently. The next night, Charles Allen and Thomas W. Gorman bagged their own saucer sightings. On July 8 Nina Warner, her son Richard, and a friend, Gladys Bolyer, both 19, saw a silvery egg-shaped object speed across the sky and vanish to the southwest, all in five seconds. Thomas J. Gorman and his daughter Rosemary saw an oval-shaped UFO emitting a brilliant light between 10- and 20,000 feet in the air. Donald Klipstein also saw a UFO in Chicago that day. Mabel Vinterum saw one from Martha Washington Hospital. Barney Dugan, a real estate salesman, saw a "dark" disk dance up, down, and sideways at cloud level, above

Western and Wilson Avenues. It then vanished. Peter Monte saw a disk "skimming at low altitude" at 10:20 p.m. near Wolf and Roosevelt Roads. At 12:45 a.m. on July 9, two World War II veterans, Thomas O'Brien and Timothy Donegan, saw four or five dark, round objects from just outside O'Brien's home. The UFOs were slightly illuminated by a "gaseous trail" and appeared to be at an altitude of 2,500 feet.

"There was a swish of noise, and they were going southwest at about 180 miles per hour," said O'Brien. That's a pretty poky speed for a UFO. Donegan added, "They left a blue streak."

By then sightings were being reported in every state. The Chicago *Tribune* was calling it "the great disc Mystery of the North American sky." And the mystery had respect.

Dr. Harold C. Urey, a nuclear researcher at the University of Chicago, said, "If only one or two reports had been made, I'd put it down to too much drinking. Even if a certain amount of hysteria is involved in some of the accounts, you cannot dismiss the testimony of such trained observers as air transport pilots."

The next "flap," or grouping of sightings, began in the spring of 1952. On April 26 Victor Root saw a saucer at night. At 5:45 p.m. on June 29, three air force police officers saw a bright silver, flat, oval object surrounded by a blue haze. It hovered, and then flew fast to the right, to the left, and up and down. The bizarre sighting lasted 45 minutes.

On July 3, 1952, at 11:50 p.m., Mrs. J. D. Arbuckle saw two bright pastel green disks fly straight and level, very fast. The sighting lasted only six seconds. On July 12, a U.S. Air Force captain, a weather officer, saw a reddish object with small white lights make a 180-degree turn and then disappear over the horizon. There were hundreds of other witnesses.

Here's a perfect witness: on September 2, 1952, a Mr. Turason, a radar tracker who worked ground control approach at Midway Airport, saw—over a period of eight hours—40 different radar targets flying in miscellaneous directions, at up to 175 miles per hour. At one point, two of the objects seemed to fly in formation with a DC-6 airliner.

On August 22, 1952, two air force jet fighters, directed by ground observers, chased a yellowish light over Chicago. The light disappeared from sight and from radar as the pilots started to close in on it. The pilots left the area and the UFO returned, ascending rapidly. A few minutes later the UFO or one like it was spotted by the Ground Observer Corps 20 miles to the northwest. It hovered, blinked twice, and ascended out of sight.

Pilot Ernie Thorpe and copilot H. S. Plowe saw a string of five or six white lights, and one blinking red light, flying alongside their plane on Decembr 8, 1952.

On June 25, 1953, at 8:30 p.m., a Mrs. Norbury and a Mr. Matheis saw a bright, yellow-white egg-shaped object. It had a red tail and was observed to make seven circles in the air slowly over a period of an hour and a half. A few weeks later, on July 16, Hazel McCombs saw a night-flying saucer. That same month, so too did Nick Sciurba.

Lelah Stoker saw a white, round-topped disk at 4:30 p.m. on April 8, 1954. Outrageously, the craft skimmed above Lake Michigan with a human-shaped figure suspended beneath it! Stoker watched as the craft landed and a figure in a green suit got out and walked around. After 30 minutes, the craft took off, very fast.

On August 22, 1954, a half-moon–shaped UFO was seen hovering and darting in various directions over Chicago. On August 26, 1960, Robert I. Johnson saw a flying saucer at night, from the Adler Planetarium.

At 10:20 p.m. on May 9, 1964, U.S. district court reporter J. R. Betz saw three light green crescent-shaped objects. They were the apparent size of a half-moon. They flew very fast in tight formation, from east to west, oscillating in size—and color, reportedly—but were in view for only three seconds.

At 9:25 on the night of October 3, 1962, Deputy Inspector of Weights and Measures Patrick McAley and his son were waiting to observe a satellite pass overhead. They saw a domed object cross the face of the moon, flying west. It was tipped at an angle and "seemed to be floating." Its size was much smaller than the moon's, and it appeared to be at a great distance.

From an anonymous woman comes a story that she recalls from sometime between 1963 and 1965, though she's sure it was around 9:30 a.m. on an August 1. "I was only 17 or 18 years old, and I was standing outside with my boyfriend's little brother, who was only 5 years old at the time. I was young at the time and didn't know to report this. I didn't think anyone would believe me.

"My boyfriend at the time lived on Kildare Avenue. If I remember correctly, the address was 2202, or close to it. What I do remember is that he lived close to the corner. The two [cross] streets were Tripp Avenue and Kildare. The lights were white and very bright—five lights across the sky—and they were very low. There was absolutely no sound. [They were] moving ever so slowly. When I looked up, I was so excited, I told [my boyfriend's brother] Mikie to run in and get everyone to come outside to see. He was so frightened, he cried running up the stairs. Well, by the time anyone listened to him and they finally came out, the lights had disappeared into the sky, as though the sky opened up and the lights just slipped into the darkness one by one.... I have never forgotten that night."

The week of June 30, 1996, UFOs were spotted all over Chicago. The Federal Aviation Authority (FAA) had multiple reports. The closest appeared oval-shaped, was metallic, and had a strobing light.

The night of July 19, 1972, Peter Reich saw a UFO near Lake Michigan. In 1973, on January 23, Lee Shapiro saw one at night, too. Brian Cumpler saw a UFO in May 1975. Later that year, on October 8, Cynthia Zusel saw one near O'Hare Airport.

At 10:30 p.m. on October 12, 1997, two children and an adult were driving home from a Cubs game when they saw a red light in the sky. "It was a circle of red light," said one witness. "It moved very fast. It moved, then stopped, went back the other way, stopped, and hovered for about five seconds." Then for about three seconds a light came down from the craft. The object then flew out of sight.

Three people were driving in a rural area near Chicago at 2 a.m. on November 20, 1997, when they saw a fast-moving, bright white light to the northeast. It was moving from east to west and seemed enormous.

"We pulled the car over and got out to view it better," said one observer. "The object, while it was stopped, changed from the bright white light we originally saw to a bluish blue. The object then darted off at a 90-degree angle and went straight up until it vanished."

On July 13, 1998, at 4:44 a.m., "stars" flying in formation were seen over Chicago. (For more information on this report, see chapter 4, "The 1998 UFO Wave.")

On October 23, 1998, at 9 p.m., a police officer looked up in the sky at the Little Dipper and saw at the bottom left of the formation a very bright teardrop shape. "It dove down, then pulled up and turned from white to yellow. Then it was gone," the officer told the National UFO Reporting Center—and no one else. (The officer told the center, "I'm a police officer, and I know better than to report this to anyone else.")

Five days later, at 1:50 p.m. on October 28, two Chicago room-mates saw a UFO with a ring of lights. One reported:

"Lying in bed, I noticed a bright ball in the sky that rapidly changed colors from red to blue to white. After realizing that it hadn't moved in the five minutes I examined it through binoculars and quickly called my roommate. I stuck a pair of binoculars in his hands, and before telling him what I saw, I asked him to describe what it looked like to him.

"Through the binoculars he saw five or six lights arranged in a compressed oval pattern. Through the binoculars each of these lights seemed rather faint, but with the naked eye it was very bright and im-possible to miss the colors flashing between red, blue, and white. The colors changed rapidly—more than a strobe light, even. To my sur-prise, he was seeing exactly what I was seeing. We watched it for about twenty minutes, and before we decided to give it a rest, what was orig-inally five or six lights had become one—perhaps whatever it was was moving farther away, although it seemed to hold the same position for the time we watched.

"I continued to watch it from my bed—I'm in a loft and have a ter-rific view of the sky. If I had to pinpoint an exact location of the light, I would place it at least two miles away in the southwest sky over Lake Michigan. I'm on the North Side, so I guess that would put it parallel with the Lincoln Park–Gold Coast area. It could easily have been over-looked by people on the ground, but once they saw it I guarantee it would have raised an eyebrow.

"I don't know what it was, but I definitely know what it wasn't."

At 5:20 a.m. on February 24, 1999, an anonymous witness reported that while looking to the north-northeast, "I perchanced to see a fluo-rescent green fireball, about the size of a dime at arm's length.* Trailing it was an orange-white tail. The object descended in a graceful arc at approximately a 45-degree angle across the north-northeast skies. There was no noise at all. I am familiar with fireworks, and I assure you this was not a firework by any stretch of the imagination. There were no other witnesses."

All these sightings may be fascinating stuff for the statistician. But the skeptic's cry for hard evidence has not yet been answered, at least in Chicago—though there was one close call.

---

* This "arm's-length" comparison may sound strange to newcomers to the UFO field. It was established by Air Force investigators to judge relative size.

On the morning of July 10, 1947, Ralph S. Waterbury found what appeared to be a flying saucer in his front yard, in Arlington Heights. It turned out to be a seventeen-inch phonograph record, similar to those broadcasters used before magnetic recording tape was available. Fastened to it were two insulators, two ceramic condensers, and a piece of radio-frequency tuning equipment.

So we must look outside of Chicago to find the proof that science demands. For example, it is a fact that in 1947 the Air Force analyzed the pieces of a flying saucer that had crashed into an Illinois farmer's field just a few tollbooths from Chicago, near Danforth, burning vegetation all around to a "fine ash."

The official results of the analysis were: "Plaster of Paris fragments, part of an outmoded magnetic speaker diaphragm, Bakelite [plastic] coil forms wrapped in enamelled copper wire, a metallic box, the remains of an electronic condenser manufactured in New York City, and the vestiges of a metallic magnetic ring. Of such things are some of the saucers made."

But this is not all saucers are made of—at least in Illinois—as we shall see.

CHAPTER 2
"TWO BEINGS WERE LEAVING MY BEDROOM"

More than 2 million Illinois residents may have been subjected to the alien-abduction phenomenon. Consider this report: "I woke up around 4 in the morning, and two beings were leaving my bedroom. They exited in a way that really troubled and disturbed me. I woke up sitting upright in bed; my body was literally vertical. They exited through a wall window. I could sense them getting into a craft outside the window. I did not see it, but it made a low-frequency hum."

The man is a Chicago professional. I'll call him Jim. The year was 1976. Whenever I speak to him about the incident, he does not sound fearful or troubled, even though he has been visited by the figures many times since. They come to his home every six to eight weeks. If anything, Jim sounds happy—happy to have someone who will listen and not judge.

And it is very hard not to judge. The reader by now will be used to UFOs violating Newtonian physical laws, such as those governing inertia. We are even used to their speeds violating the light-speed physics outlined by Einstein. But the abduction phenomenon calls into question our entire perception of reality, with one theory calling for the beings to exist here, on our planet, right now, but occupying a different plane of existence. They perhaps occupy the area between the electron and neutron and nucleus—quite a large "Twilight Zone," actually, considering the size of those particles: an atom is mostly empty space.

Or not.

What do we do with the abductees?

Even within the broad spectrum of unexplained phenomena, their stories are, well, impossible! Just as scientists wish UFOs would go away, so too do many UFO researchers wish the abductees would go away.

It is all a matter of perspective, and point of view is never so varied as when dealing with the abduction phenomenon. Some "victims" prefer not to be called "abductees" but "experiencers." Those responsible are not "aliens" but "visitors." And the experience itself—being probed and poked, having one's eggs or semen collected to create human-visitor (alien) hybrids within a human woman's womb (without permission), only to be later retrieved by the visitors (without permission)—all of this is not "bad," but is a necessary assisted step up into a higher plane of human existence.

Dr. John Mack of Harvard University argues that the phenomenon is real but not real. That is, some outside force enters the experiencer's consciousness and carries out the perceived activities there, not in our physical world at all. And some, as outlined previously, say that the visitors merely have a different atomic vibration and are sharing the planet at this moment. This, perhaps, explains the range of extrasensory-perception abilities some experiencers report—the experiencers have become accustomed to different levels of reality, where only quantum physics applies.

"I've had experiences with everything," said Jim. "Premonitions, mind-reading—things like that. Not enough to—you know—but I knew I was different."

Arguing against the "all-in-the-mind" theory are the very real scars left by the visitors and the inexplicable "implants" that have been removed in a few cases from the experiencers' physical bodies. There have even been a few medically documented pregnancies that—well, the women must have spontaneously aborted and not even known it. They *must* have.

Some researchers, myself included, refuse to classify the tales as UFO encounters but rather set the stories next to reports of mysteriously slaughtered cattle and call the reports "human mutilations." What else could one call the bizarre genetic experiments carried out in curving, windowless rooms with no corners and no doors?

And what *about* those genetic experiments? Here are the visitors, working in our air and gravity—working with our blood, even, in a day when your dental hygienist wears rubber gloves—without fear of contaminating themselves or humanity. The *Apollo* astronauts had to be locked up in a trailer home for days for fear of moon germs. If nothing else, this is proof that the aliens are not literary: this is what killed the Martians in *War of the Worlds*. It's what destroyed humanity in *The Andromeda Strain*.

And if the visitors have mastered time or space or both to cross the immense voids between their homes and ours, why are they still messing around with experimental subjects? Even our own fledgling science of genetics has advanced to the point where a few cells are sufficient for research. We don't need to come back to the same experimental subject for decades, subjecting generations of the same family to tests. Nor does genetics need a womb.

And an alien race would hardly have DNA compatible to our own. In fact, there is no reason to believe that they would even *have* such a thing as DNA with which to pass on inherited traits. The proteins that make up amino acids seem to be a universal constant—they're found in meteors—but evolution somewhere else could hardly be expected to craft them into compatible DNA, or even DNA at all. The visitors do seem more human than inhuman, however; heights and colors and the number of fingers change in reports, but they do have fingers. And they always have two hands, two eyes for binocular vision, two arms, two legs, and a mouth.

For this reason, some have suggested that the visitors are actually oddly evolved humans from the future. Others say they are characters from a parallel reality, or even angels (it gets New Age-y fast in this field). Still others say that the whole exercise is designed merely to provoke our reaction: it's an alien sociology experiment.

The visitor/New Age/angel school says that the visitors are benign, benevolent, and extremely committed to the spiritual growth of the human race. They tampered with the cave men and women to help them evolve, and they're doing it again. If they experiment with our bodies, it is to set our physical plant aright, so that we may tap into the energies that will allow us to evolve into our next stage of being. The visitors are angels; but our angels—those angels—have always been angels, have been falsely identified over the millennia and only now are seen as our alien friends. Even if false, such beliefs allow the experiencers to integrate the incidents into their daily lives. Far from being victims, they are God-touched.

Conversely, researchers with a fundamentalist Christian bent call the creatures demons, similarly misidentified over the centuries as vampires, succubi…Satan. (I do not know if there is a Satan, but the visitors will answer until he comes along. If the events reported have any truth at all, then the grays are evil incarnate.)

That said, there is no denying that most of those who claim to have been carried off by the "grays"—the slight, nude figures with the slender limbs, teardrop heads, and wraparound eyes most often reported—are tormented by their very real but uncertain memories, which their minds sometimes, not always, force into the subconscious. (Contrary to popular belief, there are many abductees who recall the experience without hypnosis. Others recall the experiences in dreams. And of course there are others whose shadowy and vague recollections are crystallized only before the clinical hypnotist.)

Abductees almost uniformly present no indications of mental disease, save for the stress associated with the abduction experiences themselves. They come from all economic classes, all ages, all races, and all political and religious persuasions. Many abductees are frightened and ashamed, coming forward with their stories only after careful deliberation.

"If someone comes over to my apartment, I'd make sure certain books were hidden," said Jim.

The most famous experiencer is horror novelist Whitley Strieber, who in 1987 wrote a book, *Communion*, about his own abductions. It offered much-needed support for others who lived in denial and also popularized what once was a dim and embarrassing corner of ufology. Then he recanted the story. Then he recanted the recantation and wrote more books on the subject. Arguing against the truth of his experiences is the fact that Strieber's reports are bizarre even within the context of abductions.

The best abduction stories have a sameness across hundreds of experiencers (and there are hundreds, if not thousands). Typically, the subject has had UFO encounters for decades, similar to those of the woman living between the Illinois communities of Orangeville, Lena, and McConnell, who at 7 p.m. on February 3, 1999, had only the most recent of many UFO sightings that have plagued her life. I'll call her Anna.

In her first sighting, when she was a girl, Anna saw three UFOs, in a triangular formation. She has seen them repeatedly in the last two years; in July 1998, her husband saw them, too. Anna describes her last sighting:

"About 7 p.m. I was walking from the front room into the kitchen area. I noticed through the window (facing the west) a very bright light that I have continuously seen all through my life. I didn't want to scare my children, so I had my husband look into the night sky. There were two of them off into the west sky, one close to the other. They were turning around and around, and the lights of the two were a bright white, and then green sparkle shimmer.

"They were constantly bobbing around, which I assume is because of communication. We watched for a while, and after about an hour they started to phase out of sight and eventually were gone. They always appear in that area, and have since I've been a child.

"My one child claimed to me that in the middle of the night he was awoken by bright lights by his window. I don't want him to be scared like what I have been all these years, so I told him it was just probably car lights coming off the road."

To the researcher, this is all very familiar: the repeated encounters, the interest shown by the visitors in all generations of a family. The next step would be to question the woman in an attempt to discover periods of missing time. If she did have such memory lapses, relaxation therapy or clinical hypnosis by a trained professional might be employed to recover lost memories—though this method is growing increasingly controversial.

Some experiencers simply do not want to recall anything. They are happier not knowing and actually fear remembering. Take the following story, from an experiencer I'll call Al. Al lived in a small town near Peoria:

"I will try to tell you what happened without any added assumptions or personal feelings to cloud the actual event. I will describe the place first to give you an idea of where in the house it took place.

"This was about 26 years ago, 1973, give or take a few months. It was hot; my dad opened all the windows to cool down our house. It happened in the upstairs of this house. The staircase began at the back of the house and angled upward to the front. At the top of the stairs on the immediate right was my room. On the left was my brother's room that had an annexed small playroom that had two windows. It also faced the front of the house. Right below the two windows was a ruffled rain roof. It was also over the front door and extended over the porch. It was supported by two decorative metal posts. I'm sure it was a scrolled-vines design.

"It was nighttime. Everyone in my family had gone to bed. I was five. My brother was seven. I woke up. Some noise was coming from my brother's room. I assumed it was him and ran right into his room. I then stopped dead. The first and only thing that got my attention were two figures standing on the rain roof. I was looking at them through the windows about 5 feet away. They were about 6 inches taller than me.

"In proportion to the rest of the body the arms were thin. I was very frightened. I stood there for a moment to look at the face of the one on the right. Its head was slightly larger. The eyes were a large, round almond shape, but they didn't slant up at the end. The one on the left began to move; I backed out of the room. I wanted to run downstairs to tell my parents, but the stairwell seemed even more dark and frightening.

"I ran back into my room and hid under my bed. I tried to be quiet. That's all I remember of that night. I woke up the next day under my bed. I didn't remember going to sleep. I know that this was not a dream. I would have remembered calming down. If it was a dream, I would have woke up in my bed and not under it, and no, I don't sleepwalk. I know what I seen.

"Over the years, I didn't say too much about it. When the subject of UFOs or alien abductions became a topic, I usually changed the subject or said nothing and listened. Even though this happened, I never associated it with an abduction because no real memory exists of an abduction. I refused to believe that it was anything more than the fact that I surprised them. They were afraid I would alert someone to their arrival, and I got zapped or tranquilized.

"Some recent issues about this keep coming back that lead me to believe that perhaps it was more than this. But I don't know. Maybe it was because the whole 'alien' thing has become a part of pop culture and I think that seeing it everywhere has influenced me to have false dreams of the beings I did see. I'm not having happy dreams about them.

"Sure, you might say, see a hypnotist about what might have happened, but I don't believe in hypnotists. I do not claim to have seen a UFO or any other aliens. If I really wanted to pursue this, I would want to see a real doctor, to check for real evidence. I am choosing not to at this time. I also wish to remain anonymous, at least for now. I haven't met anyone who has had an experience like mine.

"I asked my brother, after it happened and a few more times over the years, and he still claims no knowledge of this event. This is one of the reasons I never tell anyone. The only other person there doesn't remember anything. I thought about asking him again. But what good would it do? He might have just been asleep.

"I couldn't confirm or deny anything that might have happened beyond this. I only know what I know. I don't in any way want to confuse the real events."

Al clearly is happier not knowing more than he already does. But if he is like countless abductees who began with such an account and then recovered lost memories, he is an abductee. "He certainly does fit the paradigm to a certain degree," said Jim, the experiencer introduced at the beginning of this chapter. "I can assure him that they weren't on the roof to inspect the roof. They were interested in both boys, probably, and his not having any memory past the event would tend to confirm that."

Jim's 1976 encounter, when he woke to see two visitors—classic "grays"—leaving his room, was just the first that he consciously recalled. He went on to work with abduction researcher David Jacobs, who is a professor of history at Temple University. Together they recovered memories of abductions going back to Jim's childhood.

He does not fear the encounters. "The human race is at a crossroads now," Jim said. "We have not and are not learning from our past. We haven't created a better world. And think that perhaps there is something in our galaxy which is intelligent, which has had an overview of us since we climbed out of the oceans."

But these are neither angels nor demons, Jim said. "Demons are never alleged to have flown in highly mechanized transport," he noted.

A strange visitor to one possible alien abductee's bedroom is recalled in this sketch, drawn by the witness to the 1973 encounter near Peoria. Some "visitors" are said to wear tight-fitting clothes, some wear robes, and others appear to be naked. This figure seemed to wear a sort of geometric carapace. It was a few inches more than 4 feet tall. Used with permission of the artist.

The interest the grays have shown in Jim centers on his reproductive system, his spine, and brain. He has never seen them speak or even seen their mouths move. As is the experience of almost all abductees, the grays communicate with him telepathically, by staring deeply with their large, unblinking eyes. "It's the deepest, shiniest black. They look deep into your mind, and they can access all of your memories, all of your thoughts. I know that sounds like a science fiction movie, but it's

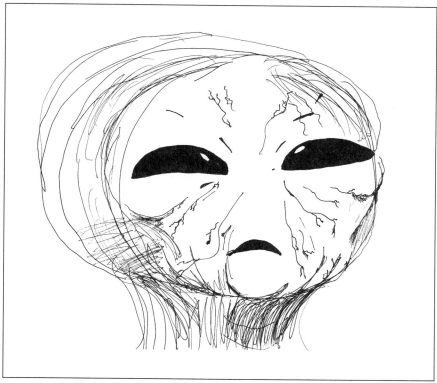

In another sketch drawn by the witness, the details of one of the figures' wrinkled heads is shown in greater detail. Used with permission.

true. They can control all of your bodily functions by looking into your eyes." Jim suspects that this has led to a lifelong social flaw he has had.

"All my life, I didn't look into people's eyes, and people have noticed it," he said. Even today it is difficult for him to do so. He was relieved to find in working with Jacobs that it was a habit many abductees share.

In Jim's experience, the grays are working on his body, studying him as an individual. He has also seen another classic type of visitor, the tall, blond "Nordic," which he says is a gray-human hybrid.

"From what I've seen," Jim said, the grays are "looking to splice pieces of us into them and create hybrids who are probably among us now, who will be increasingly filtered into society."

In fact, he says, the grays themselves are perhaps a hybrid race, bred by the taller grays that sometimes are featured in abductee accounts as leaders. While strongly resembling grays, they tend to have more of an insect look, something like a praying mantis.

Jim himself has never cared to have children. Now he suspects he may know why. According to the grays, he is already the father of many...hybrids. "They showed me images of kids in a park, in a very natural sort of area. They did have features similar to mine. But they did have almond-shaped eyes. And there were *dozens* of them. It was like tons of them, and it really freaked me out."

Jim suspects that the genetic engineering might have good side effects: cancer could be bred out of the human race, for example. But Jim has suffered from chronic sinusitis for years.

"One of my two nostrils was so blocked by scar tissue," he said, it mystified his doctors. But the grays are well known to insert implants in this area. And Jim also suffers nosebleeds and unexplained scars "constantly."

"My bedsheets constantly have blood on them," he said. "It's quite a problem."

He has learned to compartmentalize his life, to put his nighttime encounters on a back shelf while he goes on with the day's activities. "And I kind of wonder how many people around me do as well," he said.

Indeed; a 1991 Roper poll showed that 18 percent of U.S. citizens—more than 2 million Illinois residents alone—have had unusual or paranormal experiences that characterize abductees: 18 percent awakened feeling "paralyzed, with a sense of a strange person or presence or something else" in their room; 13 percent experienced a period of time of an hour or more in which they were apparently lost, but could not remember why or where; 10 percent felt at some time the sensation of actually flying, though they didn't know where, why, or how; and 10 percent saw unusual, unexplainable light or balls of light in a room. Most unsettling, 8 percent—or almost 900,000 Illinois residents—reported discovering "puzzling scars" on their bodies that neither they "nor anyone else" remembered being inflicted.

I suppose 900,000 Illinoisans could be mystified by a bruise or a cut, but a wound so deep that it causes a scar? Every one of them is lying or mistaken—or else there is something unusual going on here.

Especially frightening to me is Jim's description of the changing social structure that will occur once the hybrids have successfully infiltrated human society.

"Once a hybrid was teaching this class," he said. "A lot of people who have this experience are taught these classes with a gray teaching them in these amphitheaters that fit about 30 people. They're just really tight and intimate, shaped like ice cream on an ice cream cone. They teach you things. They tell you things that you're going to need to know in your future. There was this hybrid teaching, and the room was all full of men my age. And I look at the [hybrid] guy and I ask him, 'What gives you the capability to teach *us*? Who appointed *you*?'

"And I'll never forget. He looked at me, and he looked back at the guys. Two or three of the guys in the audience got up and turned to me—it was so mechanical. And they all [telepathically] spoke to me in unison: 'It's not so much me telling you as it is a universal truth. Your thoughts and experiences belong to the group, not the individual.'"

So a sort of hive mentality awaits us, perhaps, where individuality will count for nothing. But Jim doesn't fear that. In fact, he said, if the grays would just come to his door and ask for his assistance, he'd probably go along with them.

"For the grays, their existence depends on it. How can you fault someone for that?" he said.

Bad science would have us dismiss the abduction phenomenon because the theorized cause is impossible. But good science accepts that at least the experience of a phenomenon and its effects—in this case, the shame, fear, and stress—are real, and possibly widespread. While Jim does well with those emotions and has come to terms with his experiences, he does have one fear.

"These have been encounters I've had my whole life, and probably I won't find the answers to anything until I'm dead," he said.

"I fear that."

CHAPTER 3
THE 100-YEAR-OLD UFO

Before the airplane, even before the blimp or dirigible, an Unidentified Flying Object was seen by thousands across all of Illinois during a monthlong wave of sightings that even today is impossible to explain.

Politicians, newspaper reporters, and clergy all saw it; in Chicago it was even photographed. But this was no misidentified airliner or advertising plane—not in April 1897!

People have seen strange things in the sky since Biblical times, coming up with explanations that fit their cultures. It wasn't until just after World War II that extraterrestrials were suggested as an explanation. Just 50 years before that, hovering cigar-shaped objects were assumed to be man-made inventions, something like dirigibles. But while a crude, experimental dirigible flew successfully in France in 1882, a practical, maneuverable craft was not yet on the scene.

The sightings began in late April 1896 in California and gradually spread east, in an apparently well-organized tour of the country. Telegraphs spread the reports to newspapers everywhere. It was a national sensation, though today it is strangely forgotten. Soon after an exhausting number of appearances in Illinois, the "airship" simply disappeared.

"In major cities like Sacramento, Omaha, and Chicago, thousands rushed into the streets or clambered to rooftops to view the vessel as it passed," wrote Daniel Cohen in his history of the phenomenon, *The Great Airship Mystery*.

One of the first mystery airship sightings occurred on the night of November 22, 1896, in Sacramento. Walter Mallory, a deputy sheriff, described it as "a strong white light" with a dark body immediately over it. At 1 p.m. the airship was sighted in Tacoma, Wash. A half hour later it was seen in San Jose, California, 750 miles away. The next evening it was in Los Angeles. Sightings continued all over the state.

William Randolph Hearst's *San Francisco Examiner* crowed on November 28, "The biggest problem of the age has been solved. Man has won his hardest battle with nature. A successful airship has been built."

By February 2, 1897, the airship had traveled inland to Hastings, Nebraska. Three days later it was 40 miles south, in Invale, Nebraska. On March 27 it was in Topeka, Kansas, where it was seen by several hundred people, including the state's governor.

Chicago eagerly awaited the visit of the airship, but then as now lights in the sky sparked fears of global governmental conspiracies. On April 1, *The Chicago Tribune* reported, "Some will have it that the machine is sent out by the British Government filled with spies, who are gathering information about our military and naval resources that will enable England to swoop down upon us as soon as she gets ready."

The British spies, or whoever, got their first glimpse of Illinois on April 3, when the airship overflew Evanston and a few other communities. It had come close to Chicago but apparently turned away. It returned to Evanston on April 9, and this time Chicago was the next stop.

On that night, at about 8:15 p.m., it was seen by 500 people in Evanston. "It was first seen at about 8:15 o'clock [sic] very low down on the horizon and had the brightness of 50 ordinary streetlights," said the *Evanston Index*. "It was in plain view for fully 45 minutes. A great many people viewed it with opera glasses, and at the life saving station they watched it for half an hour with their large glass, and were certain it was the famous airship about which so much fun has been made in the papers."

In Evanston, according to the *Chicago Times Herald*, one witness described the airship as "being composed of two cigar-shaped bodies attached by girders." Another witness, who had watched through binoculars, "was able to discern four lights a short distance apart and moving in unison. The first was a bright white light and appeared to be operated like a searchlight. Behind it was a green light and farther to the rear were green and white lights closely set together."

Other witnesses believed they could see wings and even sails. Still others scoffed. Professor G. W. Hough of the Dearborn Observatory in Evanston, who admitted he had not bothered to look at the airship through his telescope, said that it was merely the star Alpha Orionis.

The airship was already visible to Chicago by 8 p.m., and it lingered there until 2 a.m. "Thousands of amazed persons declared that the lights seen in the northwest were those of an airship, or some floating object, miles above the earth.... Some declared that they could distinguish two cigar-shaped objects with great wings." *The New York Herald* also reported that Chicagoans saw, from time to time, the beams from the airship's two great searchlights.

The airship stayed in the Chicago area for three days, long enough to be photographed. At 5:30 a.m. on the 11th, news dealer Walter McCann was picking up his newspapers at the Northwestern Railway depot when he saw the airship approaching from the south.

"It looked like a big cigar," McCann said. "It came nearer and I saw at a glance that it was not a balloon. Quick as a flash I realized it was the much talked of airship. My boy won a camera not long ago in a contest for getting subscribers to a paper. It was in the store, 50 feet from where I stood gazing at the object. I ran and got it as the thing approached. The sky was clear. Conditions favored a good photograph. A plate was ready. I ran to Greenleaf Avenue and Market Street and got a good shot at it. With G. A. Overocker, whose attention was attracted to it, I ran down the Northwestern tracks and we got a second picture a few minutes later."

Other witnesses to McCann's photographing were E. L. Osborne and William Hoodless, a member of the Salvation Army, which then even more than now was known for its extreme devotion to religious principles and the harsh sacrifices required of its members.

This is a newspaper etching made from an early UFO photograph allegedly taken in Chicago by Walter McCann on April 11, 1897. Sadly, the original has been lost. Courtesty State Historical Society of Wisconsin.

Surprisingly to skeptics, McCann gave copies of the photo to all newspapers that requested it, and he refused to sell the negatives. "I have lived here too long to try to fool people. I have no desire for notoriety," McCann said.

Sadly, the photos have been lost, though an engraving of the second picture, produced for newspaper reproduction, has survived.* It was published in the April 12 *Chicago Times-Herald* and is reprinted here. The paper's staff artist and etcher subjected the photos to acid tests and said the photos were authentic. The *Tribune* and the *Post* said the camera's field of vision was too small to have captured the airship and the foreground objects—though both papers admitted that they had not examined the camera or even knew what make and model it was.

---

* I think it extremely likely that the photo survives, in the hands of Mc Cann's descendants or perhaps in the "morgues" or libraries of Chicago newspapers that later folded; it was and is typical for papers to donate their retired collections to schools or libraries. If any curators of such a collection should find the photo, I would certainly like to hear about it.

Whatever it was, the airship had a crushing schedule, visiting dozens of Illinois cities and towns in less than 25 days, suggesting a single fast-moving craft or an entire fleet of airships. Usually it was perceived only as a strange light moving in the sky. Twice, "messages" supposedly dropped from the airship were recovered, but as they are almost certainly hoaxes, I do not include them here, nor do I include obvious misidentifications of Venus or of balloons with dangling candles, launched by pranksters (a practice that sadly continues, with improved technology and striking effect, today). For those incidents for which I have witnesses' names, I provide them here.

The Illinois tour had begun slowly. On April 3, 1897, the airship was seen in Evanston and Rochelle. On the 5th it was seen in Nashville. On April 8 it was seen by James H. Clark in Dixon; it was seen also in Rock Island and in Sterling.

April 9 was an exceptionally busy night for the airship. it was seen in Aurora; in South Chicago; by a Mr. Younger in Elgin; in Evanston; in Goodrich; in Jerseyville; by R. D. Sherman in Kankakee; in Morris; by Owen McGinnis in Mount Carroll; again in Rock Island; by George Clem in Skokie; again in Sterling; by Jack Connell in Sycamore; and by Mrs. W. E. Andrews in Taylorville.

On April 10 the airship still kept up its aggressive schedule. It was seen by R. W. Allen in Chicago; in East St. Louis; in Edwardsville; in Jacksonville; in Kewanee; by William Allen in Kinmundy; in La Harpe; in Moline; by J. Donner Diffenbaugh in Monmouth; by Charles Lutter in Nora; by William Trabing, Sr., in Ottawa; and in Quincy, where the *Whig* newspaper reported, "Men who saw the thing describe it as a long, slender body shaped like a cigar, and made of some bright metal, perhaps aluminum, on which the moonlight glistened. On either side of the hull extending outwards and upwards are what appeared to be wings, and above the hull could be seen the misty outlines of some sort of superstructure, a clear view of which, however, was intercepted by the wings." In front was a searchlight, and halfway back were a green light on the right side and a green one on the left, similar to water vessels' running lights. One witness said he thought it was about 70 feet long, another put it at twice that, and still another said it was not more than 50 feet in length.

Activity seemed to wane a bit on April 11, when it was seen by Count Ferguson in Arcola; in Aurora; in Bloomington; by Herman Fry in Chicago; in Decatur; in Elburn; in Elgin; by W. D. Hall in Harvard;

by F. W. Alex in Lake Forest; in Moline; a second time in Rochelle; and by Harry Defweller in Waukegan.

On April 12 it was seen by Hardy H. Whitlock in Bismarck; by F. L. Bullard from Western Avenue in Chicago; in Clinton; by Paul Mc-Cramer, two miles south of Girard; by Ed Sterrett in Henry; by John Fitzgerald from Pulaski Street in Lincoln; in Moline; from William Street in Nilwood; in Orion; by Charles P. Malley in Perry; in Sherman; by W. C. Brown in Sterling; and in Williamsville.

After such a busy night, on the 13th the airship visited fewer communities. It was seen in Canton; in Dixon; for the third time, by Robert Solomon, in Rock Island; and by Jake Breitenstein in Warsaw.

On April 14 it was seen by Peter Demuth and Elmus Clapp in Alton; by Jim Dinkerson in Andalusia; in Carlyle; in Carrollton; in Cuba; in Hillsboro; by James Hammond in Le Roy; by F. H. Geyer, for the third time, in Sterling; again by Jake Breitenstein in Warsaw; and in Peoria, where the *Transcript* reported that it was seen by thousands of reputable citizens. "The first acknowledgment of its presence was a strange light in the sky, some say about 1,000 feet high, and variously described as in size from an incandescent electric light to three times as large as a locomotive headlight." But this time there were few descriptions of the airship's "hull," and there were certainly no wings seen. It also seemed to bob and meander instead of following a set course.

Attorney David Coningdsky said it looked to him like a balloon sent up as a joke, and he was right. It was a *Transcript* hoax: three paper hot-air balloons with makeshift lanterns under them. It was a disappointment, but the next day brought exciting news: the airship was explained!

A Madison, Wisconsin, newspaper had pointed out that the airship's appearance in Chicago occurred "almost simultaneously with the advent to that city of the Ringlings." One of the brothers was even observed transporting "large and mysterious bundles" from the circus grounds. A reporter sent to the Ringling circus's winter quarters in Baraboo, Wisconsin, found that residents there were "of the opinion that the airship was a succession of balloons or something of the kind, which were aimed to prey upon the curiosity of an incredulous public to the end that shining half dollars would pour into the big wagons where tickets for the big show are sold."

The controversy was stirred by Chicago attorney Max L. Hasmer (or Kasmer; accounts vary). Hasmer was secretary of the Chicago

Aeronautical Association, and he told the *Chicago Tribune*, "Yes, I have a good idea concerning all this mystery. I know one of the men who is in the airship. The car contains three people, but the exaggerated stories concerning the ship are laughable." In fact, Hasmer said, the Association's president, Octave Chanute, had been one of the project's investors.

And so on April 15 the *Chicago Times-Herald* stated that the airship was definitely the product of the Ringlings' Baraboo workshops, where it was still being tested and perfected. The article said that the airship was based on a model created by a New York inventor, built by a man named Carr, and further developed by the Ringlings. Ringling Bros. denied it, and so does a leading circus historian today.

"I've never heard of any dirigible experiments with the Ringling show," said Fred Dahlinger, Jr., director of the circus library and research center at Baraboo's Circus World Museum, housed in the very Ringling workshops where the airship allegedly was created. Today the old winter quarters are a state-owned and -operated historic site. "I really would find it hard to believe that any show at that time would do anything with dirigibles," he told me for my book on Wisconsin's unexplained phenomena, *The W-Files*.

Despite the news on the 15th of the airship's invention, that night it was seen by Robert Hitch in El Paso; by Charles P. Malley, making his second sighting in Perry; again in Quincy; by Adolph Winkle two miles north of Springfield; and by another witness on Monroe Street in the same city.

The 16th saw a marked drop in the airship's schedule. It was seen only by William Walmsley south of Minonk; in Mason City; in Rankin; and in Vandalia.

On the 17th it was seen by a Mr. Starks in Metropolis, and on the 20th by a Mr. Everhart in Havana. On the 18th it was seen by Vernon Allen in Sycamore. On the 19th it was seen by Aaron Watson in Galton and by M. G. Sisson in Greenville. On the 23rd Ollie Kellogg saw it in Saint Joseph. On the 25th came the last airship sighting in the state, when George Smith observed it in Rossville. He would be one of the last to see it anywhere. After a few appearances in Indiana, the airship's eastward tour appeared to have ended.

But the airship would return. Its crew apparently weren't satisfied with their reconnaissance. And the next time we wouldn't fear British spies... but creatures from another world.

CHAPTER 4
THE 1998 UFO WAVE

"I am not suggesting anything grand or spectacular. I am only reporting what I have witnessed. I hope to somehow find the answer to this curiosity that has crossed my path twice."
—Anonymous UFO observer in Bedford Park

"Next week we are going to sleep out again with cameras, and if anything happens I will write back."
—14-year-old boy in Woodstock

"I've never seen a UFO to my knowledge. This is the first time for my wife, too. I'd love to think that what we saw was alien."
—Man in Chebanse

"I don't know why I stopped to look up at that star. Maybe I felt like I was being watched. I know that sounds crazy."
—UFO observer in South Beloit

Each of these people, and many others, in the spring of 1998 saw something in the Illinois sky that they could not explain. At first, some thought they were seeing a star. Some thought they were planes. One man thought that what he had seen must have been a plane struck by lightning! The point is that none of them was expecting to see a UFO, and in most cases the witnesses only hesitantly concluded that they were seeing something odd. After the fact, one person marveled at his calm demeanor during the entire event—while his cousin panicked.

Still, in the spring of 1998 they could well have expected to have seen a UFO, especially beginning at 9 p.m. Only in retrospect is it clear that the state was enjoying (or suffering) a UFO flap, or wave of sightings.

There were sightings before and after the April–May wave, as well as a brief July encore. But those other events were not jammed so densely into the calendar.

It began in Bedford Park, at 12:25 p.m. on April 4, 1998. "I had just got out of work and was waiting for my brother to pick me up," one man later told the National UFO Reporting Center. "I glanced up at the sign on our storefront, when I noticed a green sphere beginning to streak above. As it was streaking, it left a white trail [contrail] behind it that elongated as the green sphere advanced."

The sphere had a white, rectangular light behind it. "Then suddenly the sphere gained velocity and vanished. Upon gaining speed, the white tail shrank and disappeared along with it. I have seen shooting stars before, but never like this. I was curious as to what it was."

The next day, at about 9:35 p.m., the man was walking with a friend. "We were talking as I glanced straight ahead and saw the same sphere streak by ahead of us, not above us. Like the first instance, it also headed west and lasted only three to five seconds.... I could not believe that I was seeing the same thing I had witnessed a day earlier. My reaction was that of amazement, and [this] reduced my ability to react. I only pointed the object out to my friend as it vanished. Unfortunately, he did not see it in time."

Just a little later, at 11:35 p.m., in Channahon, a young student saw a much different UFO:

"I left my friend's house to take another friend home. After I dropped him off I headed toward my house, when I noticed three lights in the sky. I was observing this over a farm field. As the road curved right, I lost sight of the object over a small wood.

"When I cleared the trees, the object was much, much closer. I was able to tell the three lights were a perfect equilateral triangle. The lights continued to expand outward, as the object appeared to come closer. I slowed to see the object as it stopped and hovered beyond a neighborhood, nearby an old rock quarry. The lights rotated clockwise, then the lead light turned toward me as the object banked, as an aircraft would turn. I thought it resembled the B-2 stealth bomber. The shape of the triangle was incorrect, though. The object was equal on all sides, as the stealth has a longer base at the tail than the shorter two wings.

"As the object moved toward me, I sped down the winding road, only looking back as I could, to horrifyingly see that this object was moving parallel to my direction of travel. The road curved, and I lost sight of the object over more trees. A few seconds later I stopped to turn left on U.S. Route 6 and saw that these lights were still there. I sped around the corner as the object tilted, while still rotating, so that the bottom of the object was facing me. I drove really fast without looking back for about 15 seconds, but that time I had lost sight of it. I returned home, took out the binoculars and searched for the object, but I could not find it. All I saw was the stars and moon that had been absent before."

In Texico, at 9:30 p.m. on April 14, a woman and her two children, ages 13 and 17, were driving home. About three-quarters of a mile from home, they noticed a bright light in the sky. It seemed to follow the car, growing brighter as they got closer to home.

Her husband, at home, recalled, "When [his family] approached the house they said it was hovering, stationary, over our house. They pulled into our driveway and stopped. Then the object started to move south and passed directly over them slowly. My son ran in and told me there was a UFO outside. I ran outside and saw it, then. By then it was about 400 to 500 feet south of the house.

"We watched it continue south, maybe a quarter mile, and it turned west. It traveled maybe a mile or so, and then we lost sight of it. I took my family inside and one at a time had each one draw a picture and give me a description of the object. They were separated when they gave me this information, yet all descriptions were alike. The object was 75 to 100 feet above the ground, approximately 30 feet wide, boomerang shaped, [with] numerous lights on the bottom [blue, red, pinkish yellow, with] two bright lights on the front that you couldn't see from the bottom. It was dark in color, no shine. It was silent. When they first saw it it was hovering, then when they stopped and got out it was moving at a walking pace, and [it moved] faster as it left."

Four days later, at Glenview, it was 9:30 p.m. when a group of children saw another triangular craft. Despite one witness's apparent youth, the straightforward and undramatic nature of his or her sighting makes it credible: "We were watching a movie when one of my friends saw something out of the window. He called all of us over to look at it. A couple of days later when I was at school, someone did a UFO project and had a picture of almost exactly what we saw. It was triangular with rounded corners. It had three white lights in each corner, and then three orange, smaller lights, surrounding a white light. It basically hovered and then shot into a white blur. It also had a whitish glow around it."

In Manito, at 9 p.m. on April 25, three friends saw a light, which then broke into two disks. The disks then merged and split again into three disks. They merged once more, disappearing with a "huge flash" and a "large shrieking sound." While this apparent merging and division sounds like rather bizarre behavior, even for a UFO, it is not uncommon and has even been documented visually and on radar in sightings, but given that this is a night sighting, the disks may have joined in such close formation that they only appeared to have merged.

It was again in Manito, at 9:30 p.m. on May 6, when two UFOs, "far too complex for a plane," were sighted two miles north of town. The witness saw them again at 1:26 a.m. on May 7.

In Carpentersville, at 9:30 p.m. on May 10, an observer looked to the southeast and saw a bright circle-shaped object approaching "at a moderate rate of speed."

"It was a very bright light. The object suddenly reversed course and shot straight up at a tremendous rate, following the same path back up." The object got smaller and smaller until it disappeared from view.

At 10:12 p.m. the next day, a retired 53-year-old state police officer and a 40-year-old licensed practical nurse were watching the sky near South Holland. There was a slight haze, but that didn't keep them from watching the full moon. Then they saw four disk-shaped objects, traveling in V formation, in a north-northeasterly direction.

"The objects appeared to be luminescent, were emitting no sound and traveling at an estimated 300 to 400 miles per hour," the retired officer said later that night. The objects were in view for just 30 seconds before they reached the shoreline of Lake Michigan, where they seemed to change course to east-northeast and then faded from view.

At 9 p.m. the next night, May 12, a man was driving through severe thunderstorms to his Chebanse home.

"I was seven or eight minutes from home and out in the country," he recalled. "To my right, up in the clouds, I thought I saw a light. A ball of light the size of the moon flashed on for two to three seconds, then went out. I was thinking that a plane might have gotten struck by lightning. I know that lightning can do some strange things, and I didn't think anything of it until I got home."

When he arrived, he found his wife "freaking out" over a disk-shaped object she had seen not ten minutes earlier, in the southern sky.

"It was in the direction I was coming from, and it had been 10 minutes earlier than what I saw," said the man. "I saw only a light and then the flash. She said that what she saw had a line of lights around the bottom. It moved back and forth over the tree line, then blinked out."

A few hours later, at midnight, a South Beloit observer saw a white, round star, a circle all alone in a field of black.

The "star" got brighter and brighter, and then ascended, out of view.

"If I had [had] a camera I would not have been able to take a picture, it happened that fast," the observer said.

On the 30th, at 1:40 a.m., two 14-year-old cousins were enjoying a night of camping out in a barnyard near Woodstock. It was largely overcast, so few stars were visible, but oddly there seemed to be enough light for the cousins to see each other fine, even at that late hour. Only in retrospect would that seem odd to them.

They brought out a high-powered flashlight. "My cousin was flashing it in the sky, pointing out different stars that we could see through the clouds," one of the boys later said.

"We were talking about something, and I saw a large and bright haze in the corner of my eye. I looked up and saw a bright, greenish object in the sky. I immediately yelled to my cousin to look up in the sky."

The cousin saw the object, panicked, and started running toward the house. As he did so, the object shot away, leaving a green-yellow glow. Then, just as suddenly, the object reappeared. The whole barnyard was then illuminated. From near the house, the cousin screamed that the object was "directly on top" of him.

"I was too busy getting my shoes on," recalled the first boy. "As I was running toward the house, all of a sudden it became pitch black, and nothing was in the sky."

It was dark, far darker than it had been earlier. As would be seen, the UFOs had gone away, but only for a few months. They were back again in July.

On the fifth, at 12:34 a.m. in the clear sky over Round Lake Beach, two zigzagging "stars" caught an observer's eye.

"I knew they were not stars when I saw they were moving," she or he said. "They were brighter than any of the stars but did not appear larger than any of the stars."

They had appeared directly over the observer and traveled an arc of 45 degrees in ten seconds, after which they disappeared.

"It looked to me as if one was chasing the other. The leading light would maneuver, and then the following light would make the same maneuver, similar to playing Follow the Leader. I observed them in a zigzag pattern. When they were almost out of my view, the two lights parted and took slightly different directions."

At 10:20 p.m. on the eleventh, a similarly playful group of three starlike points appeared over Chicago. They shifted positions relative to each other but maintained a direction just slightly north of due east. The objects were silent and traveled through two degrees of an arc per second, first appearing directly overhead and then passing through the star Cygnus.

Just 20 minutes later, a yellow UFO appeared in the sky northeast of Franklin Park. It was traveling north and appeared through binoculars to be circular or spherical. It was in view for a minute before disappearing at the horizon.

On the 20th, two friends were driving east between Tinley Park and Interstate 57, on Interstate 80. It was 2 a.m. They had just had some coffee.

"I looked up toward the north and observed what looked like a low-flying plane traveling at a very high rate of speed," said the observer who reported the sighting. "But after looking at it for a while, I noticed that it didn't look like a plane at all. It was actually two lights on the bottom of some craft that blinked at the exact same time, at about three-second intervals. What was so strange is that there weren't any other lights on the craft. Also, it was going really fast. It was out of sight within three minutes."

The object followed Interstate 80 for that time, before making a sharp turn to the north, flying out of sight. "It went toward Lake Michigan, not toward the airports," noted the observer. "It just didn't look like any plane I have seen flying around here. With the two airports, O'Hare and Midway, I see planes all the time and what they look like at night. This just didn't have the normal plane or jet lights. There was also a passenger jet off in the distance, and we compared the two, and they looked nothing alike."

Why UFO reports seem to cluster in time and location is unknown. The air force found that publicity given to sightings does *not*, as one might expect, lead to additional sightings. And so the reason for Illinois's 1998 UFO wave remains unexplained.

CHAPTER 5
CLOSE ENCOUNTERS OF THE JULY FOURTH KIND

L et's say you have traveled thousands of light-years to a far-distant planet. Beneath you, beneath your craft, is a foreign civilization. It is overlaid on a great, dark semicircle, pitch black except for the dots here and there of winking, artificial lights.

As you transit the planet's dark side, you might notice that the residents' lights and structures appear to have some slight sort of intelligent arrangement. More than that you may not be able to say. An alien yourself, with a completely different thought system and perhaps different physical senses, you might not be able to recognize the right angles of the mathematically precise road markers below you. The computing machines on board or at home may later identify the lights along the paths as significant to base-ten mathematics, an obvious sign of intelligence, but at the time the thoughts of the creatures below are too different for you to perceive.

And then they begin to send up—well, they appear to be signals: explosions of light that are striking but that can pose absolutely no harm to you. Whatever this is, it is not a weapon. All around you, blossoms of light burst into color, perhaps in welcome, perhaps in warning. Do these creatures know you are here? Perhaps this is a form of communication. Curious, you descend to see if more communication will follow.

It has been your good fortune to arrive over the United States of America on July 4, and the beacons all around you have served as bait to draw you close enough to be observed—by the earthlings.

For three hours on July 4, 1997, unknown to each other, hundreds if not thousands of Illinois residents all saw a blue-green UFO or UFOs that flirted with fireworks displays.

It began with an anonymous witness in Lenzburg, at 8:30 p.m. "I was outside with my wife and daughter and her boyfriend. The sky was dark as we shot off fireworks. My wife and I were walking around our trailer, getting our dog, when suddenly a bluish light lit up the night bright enough to see everything, so bright that I kind of ducked down at first, out of reflex. As I looked up I saw a bright blue ball-shaped object moving east to west at a very fast speed, crossing nearly directly overhead. I could not tell how high it was. There was no sound. As I looked at it, it seemed to just disappear. It did not travel out of my sight but disappeared, and the night became dark once more."

At 9:15 p.m., in Elmwood, an anonymous witness watching fireworks saw an unusual object descend from the clouds. It first appeared as a bright flash. "When I looked high to the direct south, a bright light pulsed from the cloud cover above. As I observed it briefly, I could clearly see that it had a very bright blue center with a bright green aura, and a medium-length tail. It was descending at a straight 45-degree angle, with no decrease in speed or loss in trajectory. It stayed true to its descent until I lost sight of it. It disappeared behind the horizon line."

Also at 9:15, a group of people in Granite City saw the object. It was bluish green, and traveled from east to west. It was in view for only a second or two.

At 9:35 p.m. a group of relatives was passing through Fairview Heights on its to way to see the fireworks in St. Louis when they saw a blue UFO with a wispy blue tail. The relatives in the car included an ice-cream store manager from Caseyville, Illinois; his brother, a Wal-

Mart manager from Memphis; an assistant manager of the Dollar Tree Store, also of Memphis; and an eight-year-old.

It was seen at the same time over Millstadt, where one observer saw it disappear in a red flash. "I would guess that it was probably space junk burning up in the atmosphere."

At the exact same time, a similar object was seen near Belleville Community College, during a fireworks display. "Most people may have taken it for a misfired firework display," said one witness. "It was blue in color and had a very long tail. It appeared to be a meteor or space junk—or a UFO." Another witness described it as royal blue, with a teardrop shape and a white, sparkling trail, about three and a half miles away. "It was potentially observed by thousands of individuals watching the fireworks."

Another witness put the appearance at the fireworks display—or a different appearance at the same location—closer to 9 p.m. "It was a bright blue oval or circular-shaped figure." Another Belleville resident also saw it at 9 p.m., from a drive-in theater. "I was with my wife and daughter watching a movie at the Skyview Drive-In Theater. About 15 to 20 minutes into the movie the entire area was lit up by a very bright blue-green light for three to five seconds. After the light was gone, I looked outside the car but did not see anything else. Being the Fourth of July, I presumed it was some sort of fireworks. There was no sound associated with the light. The drive-in was almost full, with approximately 100 to 150 cars."

At 9:40 p.m. spectators at the Collinsville fireworks display were seeing it. One person called it a blue light and said that there was a crackling or burning sound. "It was hard to make out any definite shape due to its speed, but it traveled with a tail behind it in an east to west direction. The observers in my immediate party were between the ages of 14 to 48."

By 9:45 p.m., the object was flying over East Alton. A family there saw a bright blue-green object streak across the southern sky, traveling from east to west. The family described it as brighter than any firework display. Said one witness, "It lit up the yard for a moment—not brightly, but more so than moonlight or fireworks—slightly less than lightning. The fact that it moved so slowly and quickly made me think it was a shooting star—a close one, because of the 'thickness' of the trail. But it shifted course a little, heading more northwest than west, which I found odd. Then it disappeared."

At the same time, the object was seen again over Millstadt, ten minutes after its first sighting there. It illuminated a 2,000-square-foot area with blue light for about five seconds.

At 9:53 p.m., in Dupo, whatever it was took shape as a low-flying object with red lights, beaming a bright blue light toward the ground. It moved from south to north, perpendicular to the flight path noted by many others. "Our family was directly in the path, and as we were all illuminated blue, we looked up into the light. It moved off toward the woods north of the house and the light was turned off. Two of us saw it go off just before it would have gotten to the woods. We all discussed this strange happening at length. The object came from the direction of Columbia, Illinois, and moved off north toward Cahokia, Illinois. Our sighting was two miles east of Dupo, Illinois, on Imbs Station Road, about three-quarters of a mile west of the intersection of Imbs Station Road and Triple Lakes Road. Observers were my retired parents, two sisters-in-law (one is the wife of a U.S. Air Force Colonel; the Colonel was lighting fireworks and did not see the light), my sister, myself, and several nieces and nephews."

A meteor would be a likely culprit, except that meteors do not hang around for hours, shining lights at the ground and changing course. At 10 p.m., a blue-green light appeared over Granite City, across the Mississippi River from St. Louis. Mike Allen, 21, saw it, along with 14-year-old Richy Winters.

Said Allen: "After lighting off our last fireworks, as our last bit of ash fell, another witness and myself saw a blue-green light move across a large field of view in the sky, then disappear at impossible speed. The light was triangle-shaped, with the brightest part being the top and bottom. It appeared as if it was sitting with the lights off, then turned them on and moved at the same time. It was under the clouds, because the light from it reflected off the clouds, like lightning does. It then moved so fast in my field of view I had to turn my head to keep up with it. It wasn't moving downward or upward. It looked as if it was moving straight across the sky. We ran in to tell my girlfriend and our friend, and they were, like, 'It's the Fourth of July. It was probably a rocket.' I said, 'No way.' Then other people saw it."

At 10 p.m. a family near Alton saw a blue-green ball of light in the sky. It was not an airplane or firework rocket, or so the family claimed.

At the same time, a teardrop-shaped object was seen over Valmeyer. It was 200 to 400 feet above the ground and traveled "slightly slower than a meteorite." One of the 12 observers said that the group saw the object as they were watching fireworks a few miles distant. "The object simply appeared in the sky and was traveling from the Illinois bluffs toward St. Louis, roughly east to west. All people noticed the object, half saying it was a meteorite, the others saying it was part of a firework that had strayed. Neither of these two theories would work because (1) the object was very low as compared to other meteorites we had seen, and (2) we set up about two to three miles from the fireworks display; therefore no stray objects could have traveled that distance."

At 10:25 p.m., some people in a boat on East Fork Lake, near Olney, saw a blue-green object for about two seconds. It was "too far up to be fireworks."

In Freeburg, at 10:45 p.m., a bright blue diamond-shaped object was observed traveling from east to west very fast, with no sound. After checking, the observer found that no one had been shooting off Fourth of July fireworks at the time.

At 10:45, the object, or one like it, was also seen over Brighton. There it was seen moving east to west over a field behind a house. "The object was about the size of a soccer ball and was electric blue at the core," said one witness. "It looked to be about 100 feet above the ground and was visible for about 600 or 700 feet, and then suddenly disappeared. The total time visible to us was five to seven seconds. There was no noise associated with the sighting. The observers are between 47 and 54 years old and business owners. We have never seen anything like this. We are not under medication or have not been treated for mental illness, and both witnessed the same thing."

At 11:30, in Columbia, a "neon light blue ball passing east to west" was seen crossing the sky in a few seconds.

Finally, 24 hours later, at 9 p.m. on July 5, in Caseyville, a "glowing ball, high in the sky" was seen. With the end of the fireworks, it seemed, the visitors' curiosity was satisfied.

But one final thought: what if the UFO occupants were not drawn to the fireworks displays out of curiosity? What if they *wanted* to be seen? Wouldn't they choose the only mass outdoor event where people are supposed to look up?

CHAPTER 6
DON'T LOOK NOW, BUT YOU'RE BEING FOLLOWED

I

f we are curious about UFOs, they are just as curious about our own craft. UFOs like to follow cars.

It is a terrifying experience, especially since such a sighting is automatically a close encounter of the second kind; the UFO is interacting with the environment. In fact, it's interacting with *you*.

The most recent story I have of being chased by a UFO comes from Channahon, on April 5, 1998. You've already read about the young driver who was chased by a triangular UFO in chapter 4, "The 1998 UFO Wave." A similar story comes from Champaign. At 9:45 p.m. November 5, 1995, a woman and her nine-year-old daughter heard what they thought were sirens. They were apparently driving at the time. Then they noticed an object resembling "Christmas lights" hovering over some nearby trees. The object followed them for a while.

Another mother and child were chased in Quincy, in mid-January, 1971. A woman and her three-year-old were driving on Spring Street when her son pointed out "those bright lights over the trees."

To the left of the car was a globe-shaped object with a narrow, boxy compartment on top, which had 14 windows. The object's base was misty or clouded. It paced their car. The woman made a U-turn to park in front of her mother's house, and as she did so a beam of light shot out from one of the windows and focused on the brick walkway at her feet. The terrified woman ran into the house and alerted her mother, who also saw the craft. It hovered over a nearby house for a while, and then flew off, to the west-northwest.

Later that year, in Centralia, on the night of November 24, 1971, Sam Olli was driving to his Phyllis Drive home from his job at the Miller Lumber Company. It was overcast, so no clouds were visible. There was no wind.

Olli rolled down his car window and saw a round object with a fuzzy outline. As it came toward him, the fuzziness disappeared. At its largest, the UFO appeared to Olli to be the size of a dime held at arm's length. It slowed to a stop as Olli turned into his driveway, and then flew west faster than a jet. The duration of the sighting had been about five minutes.

Olli went inside but was then called to the door by a neighbor, Larry Patterson. Patterson had had a similar experience. He had left his accounting job at R. K. Holt and picked up his daughter at nursery school. On the way home, near Foundation Park, he saw a brilliant, glowing white-and-yellow globe hovering. It then began to move in circles, in rapid spurts. Patterson stopped briefly at Gragg Street to watch the object, and then continued on home.

To Patterson, the object had the apparent size of a pea held at arm's length; his sighting lasted about 15 minutes.

At 3:30 a.m. on August 5, 1969, Marine Corporal Charles Brandmeyer was driving between Albers and New Braden on Route 161 when he saw a small, intense light moving over a wooded area. Suddenly it made a sharp turn and headed right at him. It drew alongside of the car and paced it. It was round and shiny, with indistinct edges, and seemed to be the size of a softball. At times it tilted, revealing an "edge." It followed him to his parents' house, where he went inside and woke everyone up.

They came out and saw the departing UFO, and then got into the faster family car to chase it. The whole event lasted more than 30 minutes.

Small UFOs like this were quite common in the early modern era of sightings, roughly from 1943 to 1948, and in the first years were the rule, not the exception.

In Bartlett, early on the morning of March 7, 1967, Mrs. L. Drzonek was driving with relatives and her beagle when the party saw a disk-shaped object descend into a wooded area. It emitted a red glare. The dog "stood against the window of the car with all his hair raised in fright." Looking back, they saw a brilliant white glare that "zoomed up out of the woods and shone straight into the rear window of the car." The UFO then followed the terrified party as they drove home.

The night of August 4, 1963, while returning from a Wayne County drive-in theater, Ronald Austin and his date saw a large white object pacing their car. It was at tree-top level. Once the UFO crossed the road, ahead of the car. Austin was so terrified by the experience that he sought medical attention. Police and others in the area also saw the UFO, or one like it.

There are possible natural explanations for such phenomena, but I don't believe they cover these observers' encounters. For example, when a D. Deirmendjian was flying from Chicago to Denver on October 15, 1967, "A relatively bright spot was seen near the ground, traveling with the aircraft at what appeared to be the position for a spectacular reflection of the sun's image. That this was indeed precisely the position was corroborated repeatedly by observing that the spot became dazzlingly bright whenever it passed over a small body of water (ponds, rivers, etc.).... The spot appeared only between clouds where there might have been some tenuous haze but disappeared again in larger cloudless areas over bare terrain and vegetation." This "subsun" was almost certainly the reflection of the sun on a layer of ice crystals beneath the aircraft.

St. Elmo's fire, too, is a natural phenomenon that sometimes can "follow" an observer. St. Elmo's fire is a slow discharge of atmospheric electricity, often seen on ships' masts—lightning is a fast discharge. On May 14, 1896, a farmer in Germany was astounded to find fireballs about the size of a man's hand traveling along wire fences on both sides of his carriage. The spooked horses began to run as the fireballs hissed and crackled, but the St. Elmo's fire did not give up the chase until the fences stopped.

But natural phenomena fall far short of the described UFO-car chases. The oldest Illinois case is also the most frightening and problematic. It occurred two miles from La Harpe, at about 8:15 a.m. on January 5, 1966.

A Mrs. E. Miles saw a flash of lights in the distance while driving north on Highway 94. She at first thought it was a fast-moving plane approaching from the northwest. The object neared and was revealed to be egg shaped.

Suddenly it was hovering beside her car, just over the telephone lines. It was silvery and had a large and very bright yellowish-white light on the side facing her. Miles tried to get the attention of a couple driving just ahead of her but could not. The UFO seemed to be about as long as a Piper Cub airplane. It began to drift very slowly on its longitudinal axis, and as the other side of the craft came into view she saw a platform, 2 feet wide.

On it was a stocky, hooded figure dressed in a bulky white suit, something such as an airport firefighter might wear. He was five and a half feet tall, and his hands were covered with mittens or gauntlets. Miles could see no doors or ports or landing gear on the craft, but she did see what appeared to be a seam, through the longitudinal center of the craft. He stared at Miles with "black, staring eyes," which she said she would never forget. The craft continued to drift, concealing the figure from view. The UFO then ascended and left the area very quickly, much faster than a jet.

After the event, Miles's memory was fuzzy; she was uncertain how much time had passed, whether she'd stopped her car, or if her 1965 Mustang had stopped running. She could recall no facial features of the figure other than its eyes.

In hindsight, this sounds a great deal like the precursor to an abduction episode, right down to the "staring" behavior that impels the victim to forget much if not all of the event. Abductees sometimes spontaneously recall the events. At other times, events are revealed in dreams or—in this country—by the careful application of clinical hypnosis by trained professionals. In other countries, especially Britain, the use of hypnosis to recall abduction memories is frowned on; perhaps not coincidentally, the stories British abductees tell have marked differences from those in the United States.

CHAPTER 7
UFOS OVER ILLINOIS

I've seen hundreds of "shooting stars" and meteor
showers. But this was the first one to make me gasp
and say, "Oh, shit!" out loud.
—Belvidere witness to an August 13, 1998, UFO

llinois has had hundreds of UFO sightings. In fact, with the exception of one corner of New Mexico, the north-central part of the
United States leads the country for the highest number of reports.

What was probably the first Illinois UFO sighting in modern times
occurred on October 8, 1857. A brilliant light moved slowly across the
sky and made a loud, exploding sound. Countless more sightings
would follow.

This chapter is a catalog of every reputable Illinois UFO report I
could find, with the exception of the 1897 reports of the mysterious
"airship," which are collected in a separate chapter, as are the large
number of Chicago sightings. Illinois sightings that survived Air Force
scrutiny are given their own special section within this chapter.

To shorten what is already a lengthy list, I make use of the little scientific technology so far created for the field's study. Research into
UFOs, casually referred to as "ufology," does have a rudimentary classification system, thanks in large part to the efforts of two leaders in the
field, computer scientist Jacques Vallee, formerly an adviser to NASA,
and Illinois's own late astronomer J. Allen Hynek, chair of Northwest-

ern University's Department of Astronomy and director of its Dearborn Observatory. For many years Hynek served as a special adviser to the U.S. Air Force's UFO investigative units, Projects Sign and Blue Book. He later went on to found his own, private UFO research group, the Center for UFO Studies (CUFOS), located in Chicago.*

Both Vallee and Hynek created classification systems for the cursory discussion of what once had been summarized only as flying saucers or flying disks. For our purposes, I am using only Hynek's system.

"UFO," for unidentified flying object, is a euphemism and an acronym coined by the U.S. Air Force; it was applied by the military to objects only *before* they were studied; that is, "the UFO turned out to be a weather balloon." If, after study, the sighting still defied description, the Air Force dropped the UFO label and called it an "unknown."

In the following listings, I use the term "UFO" only in the sense that the object was unidentified to the witness; it may be that some or many of the reports have conventional explanations. However, I have not included reports that were subsequently explained or that were revealed to be hoaxes.

Hynek's two classification systems have gained a lot of currency in popular culture, without a lot of understanding. The first system describes the object's appearance:

Nocturnal light—by far the most common sort of sighting, this can look like a star or a planet, which is often what it turns out to be. It's not reserved for night but can also occur in the morning and evening, in which case Venus is a very likely suspect.

Daylight disk—this is our old friend the flying saucer, which in reality (well, the reality of UFOs, at least) comes in a bewildering variety of shapes and sizes; boomerang, triangle, cross, cigar—you name it, someone sometime has seen it. As Hynek points out, distant daylight disks may account for nocturnal lights, and it is also true that during the day some UFOs appear to be simply fast-moving points of light. Strangely, the most often reported shapes of objects change over time, with fair consistency. It's almost as if new makes and models come out; this, in fact, has been the conclusion of some Air Force personnel. These days triangular craft are reported with the greatest frequency, nearly replacing the classic domed platter.

---

* The center, located at 2457 W. Peterson St., Chicago, IL 60659, (773) 271-3611, offers a variety of publications.

Radar sighting—UFOs on radar screens are not as rare as you might think. Well, actually, these days they are quite a bit rarer than they previously were, since civilian airport radars no longer "paint" all airborne objects and return the signals. Instead, they look for the radar beacons or "transponders" aboard aircraft. But even earlier in aviation history, a radar return did not provide certain knowledge of a UFO, as temperature inversions and other atmospheric peculiarities could give a false return. Radar-visual sightings, on the other hand, with radar returns and eyewitness observation, are hard to argue against. Most military radars, of course, still paint all objects.

Hynek's second and better-known classification system ordered the proximity and behavior of the observed UFO, relative to the witness:

Close encounter of the first kind—the big necessity here is distance, just a couple hundred feet. As opposed to the distant disk-shaped light, now we can see some details and perceive depth. Therefore, stars, aircraft, etc., are almost certainly ruled out.

Close encounter of the second kind—now the UFO is seen to interact with the viewer or environment. It follows our car, avoids intercepting aircraft, or changes course in a logical manner. Landing marks may be made, grass may be charred, or debris may fall from the object—the so-called gossamer threads of "angel hair" that, theoretically, are made of ionized air sleeting off an electromagnetic field surrounding the object. The theorized field also may interfere with TV and radio reception or make vehicles stall. The skeptics' constant call for hard evidence begins to be answered here; the Center for UFO Studies has logged more than 800 of these physical-trace cases.

Close encounter of the third kind—here entities are observed, and we may now safely call the objects "craft," for they are certainly occupied, and probably even piloted by the occupants. Everything from Bigfoot to Nordic humans in ski suits have been seen in or around UFOs. Strangely, there are very few bizarre monsters. They mostly resemble humans; thus they are "humanoids." It may be that nature selects for human characteristics in all worlds where intelligence has risen. Or it may be that the "aliens" are actually humans coming back from the future. These days, no thoughtful student of UFOs jumps to conclusions. We are in the data-gathering stage and are obviously unable to test any hypothesis. Still, the most common reported alien in the United States is the "gray," a slim, naked lad with no genitalia, no nose, a swollen head, and wrap-around eyes. (In Great Britain, the most common alien is the Nordic.)

Following Hynek's death, another rank has been added, *close encounters of the fourth kind*, encompassing the abduction phenomena.

I have given extended descriptions for unusually novel sightings. In some cases I have tried unsuccessfully to find more material on certain sightings and have only the information given here.

For me, the strongest evidence in favor of the reality of UFOs comes simply from the large number of reports. Every witness must be mistaken or lying, or there is something to the phenomenon.

When a sighting report is delivered entirely as a quotation, it was drawn from the files of the National UFO Reporting Center, which has generously shared its data.

Here they are:

ALBERS, 3:30 a.m., August 5, 1969—Close encounter of the second kind. See chapter 6, "Don't Look Now, but You're Being Followed."

ALGONQUIN, January 9, 1969—Russell Hickman observed a nocturnal light.

ALMA, May 19, 1910—Myron Craig observed a nocturnal light.

ALTON, July 12, 1952—William H. Scott observed a nocturnal light.

ALTON, June 15, 1971—Tony Wilkens had a close encounter of the third kind.

ALTON, 9 p.m., July 4, 1997—See chapter 5, "Close Encounters of the July Fourth Kind."

ARLINGTON, 10:30 p.m., July 7, 1995—A man saw the "whole sky light up." The light seemed to come from very high up and was so intense that it created shadows on the ground. To me, this sounds like the flash from a meteor burning up. It's an extremely disconcerting though natural phenomenon, which I've experienced myself.

AURORA, October 12, 1958—Police Officers William Hornyan and Jack Adams saw several yellow objects moving in all directions. There were many other witnesses.

AURORA, early 1967—Ronald Kolberg saw a nocturnal light.

AURORA, March 8, 1967—Lonnie Davis saw a daylight disk. That night, William Hornyan observed a nocturnal light.

AURORA, 11:59 p.m., July 7, 1995—A man saw an object streak overhead, to the southeast horizon.

AURORA, 8 p.m., June 5, 1995—At least one witness saw a black, silent, triangular object approach and then depart.

AVISTON, November 26, 1970—At night Bob Crow saw a ball of light from Highway 50.

AVISTON, January 26, 1971—Arnold T. Wessel saw a bell- shaped object at night.

BARRINGTON, January 9, 1969—Nocturnal light observed.

BARRINGTON, August 18, 1975—Witness experienced a close encounter of the first kind.

BARRINGTON, September 26, 1975—Nocturnal light observed.

BARRINGTON, November 19, 1975—Nocturnal light observed.

BARTELSO, January, 1972—Donna Wilken experienced a close encounter of the first kind.

BARTLETT, early morning, March 7, 1967—Close encounter of the second kind. See chapter 6, "Don't Look Now, but You're Being Followed."

BARTLETT, 6:24 p.m., December 24, 1998—"I saw a cigar- shaped object with red lights and one white light on the nose. It was moving west-northwest very fast, and [then] slowed down and sped up quickly. I watched it approximately 25 seconds. It made no sound at all. We have a lot of air traffic for O`Hare, and aircraft pass [over in] only 30 seconds. My dog even stopped and watched it."

BATH, 10:15 p.m., March 1, 1996—A woman, her children, and their neighbors saw a "big orange ball of light." It dimmed and then reappeared, with a red blinking light. It left quickly.

BEARDSTOWN, 8:20 p.m., July 9, 1989—A 27-year-old railroad conductor with four years of experience in active duty as an infantry officer saw two gold circular-shaped lights in the northwest. "The first light slowly dimmed out, and then a second gold light higher than the first lit up. Then it slowly dimmed out. After four or five minutes, I saw four more lights in the northwest part of the sky, lighting up and then slowly dimming out. At one point all four were lit up at the same time. After maybe 15 minutes, I saw four more lights in the northeast region of the sky, count the same." The lights were always in a row, and no movement was perceived.

BECKEMEYER, September 1967—Mae Jannett observed a nocturnal light.

BECKEMEYER, August 1970—Debbie Tallman and others observed daylight disks.

BECKEMEYER, November 16, 1970—From the public school, Jacqueline Lanter saw a nocturnal light.

BECKEMEYER, spring 1971—Several men observed a UFO take off.

BECKEMEYER, April 13, 1971—Nocturnal light observed.

BECKEMEYER, June 16, 1971—Gerald Skiver observed a nocturnal light.

BECKEMEYER, June 18, 1971—Terry S. Turner observed a nocturnal light.

BECKEMEYER, August 25, 1971—Gerald Skiver observed his second nocturnal light.

BECKEMEYER, November 4, 1971—George Jannett observed a nocturnal light.

BECKEMEYER, January 8, 1972—Gerald Skiver observed his third nocturnal light. (It used to be that "repeaters" were viewed with suspicion; today such witnesses are questioned closely for fear that they have been subjected to the abduction phenomenon.)

BECKEMEYER, February 18, 1972—George Jannett observed a nocturnal light from Highway 50.

BECKEMEYER, September 23, 1972—Steve Garner and another witness observed a nocturnal light.

BECKEMEYER, August 2, 1972—Edward Albat and another witness saw a fireball.

BECKEMEYER, January 3, 1975—Olive Kohrs observed a nocturnal light.

BEDFORD PARK, 12:25 p.m., April 4, 1998—A storekeeper sees a green sphere with a rectangular light behind it, leaving a contrail. (For more information see chapter 4, "The 1998 UFO Wave.")

BEECHER, November 25, 1976—Nocturnal light observed.

BELLEVILLE, January 18, 1968—Kenneth A. Klamm observed a nocturnal light.

BELLEVILLE, September 1970—Maxine Frantz observed a nocturnal light.

BELLEVILLE, June 6, 1971—A housewife observed a nocturnal light.

BELLEVILLE, June 11, 1972—Paul Dorn observed nocturnal lights moving in a circle.

BELLEVILLE, July 31, 1972—John Rosenkranz observed a nocturnal light.

BELLEVILLE, 1 a.m., July 27, 1995—A man saw a silver cylinder moving in the sky.

BELLEVILLE, 9, 9:30, and 9:45 p.m., July 4, 1997—See chapter 5, "Close Encounters of the July Fourth Kind."

BELVIDERE, 4:13 a.m., August 13, 1998—Five miles north of the city, a large blue flashing object was seen. It had an "evenly split" blue tail and left a contrail. The fast-moving object was in view for only 10 seconds.

BENSENVILLE, August 11, 1972—An orange UFO was seen from Highway 83 in a close encounter of the first kind.

BENSENVILLE, July 1, 1975—Nocturnal light observed.

BLOOMINGDALE, June 24, 1976—Nocturnal light observed.

BLOOMINGTON, 6:30 a.m., February 6, 1995—Two partnered truck drivers eastbound on Route 136 were about 15 miles west of the Dixie Brothers Truck Stop. The front truck began to slow and eventually pulled off the highway. Curious, the second driver did the same. He looked out his cab and saw three "vertical slashes of light" in the sky. The central shaft of light was longer than its neighbors, and after five minutes it let out a cloud of "red dots" before all the lights disappeared. During the entire incident, there was no other traffic. The rear driver called the FAA from the truck stop, as well as the National UFO Reporting Center, which—despite the bizarre nature of this report—had similar reports from Boston and Portland, Oregon. "It was nuts," the trucker said. The emotion of the Louisiana-based driver was evident to the Center's operator.

BLOOMINGTON, 5:50 a.m., December 14, 1989—An observer was walking his dog and looked up to see two "stars" following each other.

BOLINGBROOK, 1:40 a.m., October 2, 1995—Several women saw an "orange or yellow arrow-shaped" object moving slowly to the west. It had a light on each side.

BOULDER, January 1967—Randy Hutchins had a close encounter of the first kind three miles north of the community.

BOULDER, August 1969—Duane Bright of Carlyle observed a nocturnal light southeast of town.

BOULDER, July 6, 1971—Three miles to the east, Duane Bright sighted yet another nocturnal light.

BRADFORD, 8:40 a.m., March 18, 1950—Robert Risher and his family were flying to Keokuk, Iowa. Near Bradford, Robert noticed an oval metallic disk ahead and slightly to the left of his Bonanza NC 505B aircraft. When the UFO passed underneath clouds, it continued to shine, revealing that it was self-illuminated. It left the area, approximately five miles northeast of Bradford, at an estimated speed of 600 to 1,000 miles per hour.

BRADFORD, December 27, 1950—A TWA airliner was en route to Kansas City. Just after dusk, Captain Art Shutts noticed a bright white light ahead, which flashed red and green. The object began to "wobble and swerve unsteadily." Then it began to fly back and forth from north to south, through an arc of 10 to 30 degrees, changing course violently. It appeared to oscillate slightly, as did the horizon when the UFO neared it, suggesting that the atmosphere around the craft was being distorted. This effect was especially noticed after the object had just put on a burst of speed. The UFO finally dimmed to a pinpoint and flew straight south. Then it "lurched," accelerated and flew up, rapidly, at a 45-degree angle, made nearly a 90-degree turn, and then dove and disappeared below the horizon, heading north. The sighting lasted 35 minutes.

BREESE, 11:30 p.m., December 29, 1967—Charles and Robert Grapperhaus and two other high school students were driving home from a basketball game as they watched a motionless bright light in the sky. They pulled over and got out, and felt an intense heat and heard a strange humming sound. One of the boys became frightened and ran back into the car. The heat was so strong that he could feel it inside. After about 10 minutes, the object left the area.

BRIGHTON, 9:45 p.m., July 4, 1997—See chapter 5, "Close Encounters of the July Fourth Kind."

BRIMFIELD, January 8, 1976—Nocturnal light observed.

BROADVIEW, June 21, 1976—Nocturnal light observed.

BROOKFIELD, November 16, 1976—Nocturnal light observed.

BROWNSTOWN, January 5, 1975—David Mahon experienced a close encounter of the fourth kind.

BURNT PRAIRIE, August 31, 1975—Ivan Phillips found what appeared to be landing traces left by a UFO.

BUSHNELL, September 3, 1970—Allen Robinson observed a nocturnal light near the F-S grain bins.

CAIRO, October 11, 1973—Close encounter of the first kind.

CAMBRIDGE, October 15, 1973—Gilbert Phillis Jr., Glenn McWane, and David Graham observed a nocturnal light.

CANTON, August 1, 1965—Close encounter of the first kind.

CANTON, January 24, 1971—Edward L. Sale observed a nocturnal light.

CANTON, July 21, 1971—Mike Hinds observed a nocturnal light.

CARBONDALE, April 23, 1950—Don Holt observed a daylight disk while traveling north on Highway 51.

CARBONDALE, 2:30 p.m., October 3, 1998—"On the specified date, myself and a few of my friends witnessed this flying object, which was not an airplane, helicopter, or balloon.... Myself and a friend were sitting on a couch outside of our fraternity house in Carbondale. I looked at the sky to see some birds flying around, and then behind the birds [I saw there] was a black object, not moving. It was about 1,500 to 2,000 feet in altitude, and about the size of a gumball held at arm's length. We both stood up to get a better look and could not figure out what it was. We were facing east, and it was about three to six miles away from us. The object began to move from north to south and back, in the sky. The object was also changing shape. When I say changing shape I mean it looked like a large rubber bag full of water suspended in the air, and the bag was changing shape. I have been around flying aircraft all my life, I am a pilot, and I have never seen anything like this ever. To prove to my friend and I that we were not crazy, I went inside to get some other people to witness this object. I brought out five people. They all saw it. Some [were] skeptical, but they did admit they saw something not normal. Then another friend of mine drove up and stated he saw the object from one of the dorms on campus, which is about two and a half miles from where I saw the object. The object then disappeared into the blue sky after about 20 minutes. It was a slow disappearance. It was not a quick bolt out of the atmosphere. After all this took place, about one to two hours later, an F-16 fighter jet... flew over the city of Carbondale five to seven times. There were several rumors of why the jet was flying around down here, but nothing official ever came out. The odd part of the jet is that for the four years I have been in Carbondale, I have never seen a fighter jet fly around this area. It just 'so happens' that the military jet shows up shortly after this craft was witnessed."

CARBONDALE, 9:55 p.m., October 16, 1998—A young woman saw a distant, spherical object. It had a slight green glow. It departed to the northeast. "I hope there were others in the area who saw this, too."

CARBONDALE, 10:30 p.m., November 23, 1998—"Myself and three other witnesses saw an unidentified flying object traveling in a direct path from north to south at a very high speed, slightly to the west of us. We were standing outside behind the house. The craft appeared to be glowing orange to orange-white in color and had two distinct sources of light: one light positioned on the west side of the craft and the other on the east. Both balls of light seemed to be connected to each other, but there was no distinct divider or connection between the two. However, the two sources of light appeared to be [coming] from one distinct 'aircraft.' The incident from beginning to end lasted about ten seconds. Also, from my point of view, the object was traveling at a height of between 20,000 and 40,000 feet. The most miraculous thing that we saw was the ball of light to the west pass in front of the ball of light to the east and change positions with it at full speed. In essence, the aircraft spun horizontally 180 degrees while traveling in a straight line, as if the craft suddenly spun around backward, but continued to fly in the original direction of flight at the same speed. I am a private pilot with almost 200 hours of flight time and am working on my instrument rating. I have been to the Oshkosh Air Show and have seen F-14 jets flying, as well as F-18s taking off from Springfield, as well as one F-18 flying over Carbondale a short time ago. However, I have never witnessed any aircraft traveling at the rate of the one seen tonight. I am convinced by the speed and peculiar light arrangement that the aircraft witnessed tonight was either military or totally unidentified. The lights of the craft were of one color, which does not satisfy Federal Aviation regulations of having anticollision lighting systems, strobe lighting systems, or landing light systems as required on normal civilian aircraft."

CARLINVILLE (between Carlinville and Carrollton), 10:34 p.m., January 19, 1999—"While driving after a late-evening social work appointment, I observed a large cigar-shaped object, which appeared to be a flat gray in color. The bottom of the object had red and white lights, alternately flashing. It was a cloudy night and the object was flying very low underneath the cloud cover. I was too scared to pull over, as I was the only vehicle in a basically cornfield expanse of land. The object initially was flying northbound at a rather quick pace, and then suddenly about 10 miles up the road (I was westbound), I saw the same object to my left traveling westbound, still at a rather quick speed. It was probably a mile or so away from my vehicle at all times. I watched it travel westbound for the next 8 miles or so, and then I lost it in the cloud cover. I did not roll down my window to check for any noises. I observed no interferences with my radio at all. I did not observe the object switching from northbound to westbound, so I guess it could have been two different objects. I am a professional and would never lie or exaggerate anything about something this scary."

CARLYLE, January 8, 1970—Carol Johnson observed a nocturnal light five miles south of the community.

CARLYLE, April 30, 1971—Herb Williams followed a nocturnal light.

CARLYLE, May 4, 1971—Herb Alexander and at least one other person observed a nocturnal light while traveling east on Highway 77.

CARLYLE, May 11, 1971—Jerell Garner observed a huge nocturnal light near Carlyle Lake.

CARLYLE, June 17, 1971—Nocturnal light observed.

CARLYLE, July 10, 1971—Nocturnal light observed.

CARLYLE, April 19, 1972—A woman observed a nocturnal light near U.S. Highway 50.

CARMI, August 16–17, 1978—Dee Heil observed a nocturnal light.

CAROL STREAM, March 4, 1968—Don Ryon experienced a close encounter of the second kind.

CARPENTERSVILLE, August 8, 1975—Nocturnal light observed.

CARPENTERSVILLE, 9:30 p.m., May 10, 1998—A spherical UFO was observed. (For more information see chapter 4, "The 1998 UFO Wave.")

CARTHAGE, October 14, 1970—Mrs. Raymond Todd observed a nocturnal light while traveling west on U.S. Highway 136.

CARTHAGE, February 2, 1971—Ruby Simmons observed a nocturnal light while traveling north on Highway 96.

CARTHAGE, April 21, 1976—Nocturnal light observed.

CARTHAGE, 11:30 a.m., July 15, 1995—"I was in a friend's house, in his driveway, talking. I was looking at the sky, toward the north, at around 11:30 p.m. The sky was very clear and I was looking at a group of stars that seemed to be in the shape of the Little Dipper, but it was neither the Big nor Little Dipper. This grouping of stars was much smaller, approximately one-tenth of the size. As I was looking at the stars, one seemed to just disappear, as if sucked into the darkness. I thought this was funny, and blinked, and kind of shook my head to make sure I wasn't seeing things, and when I looked up again, the place where the "star" was—or so I thought was a star—was just darkness. I looked at my friend and said, 'Did you see that?' He had not seen this, so we started to watch the sky in this area. Within a minute of seeing the star or whatever it was disappear, we both saw a light flash [that] was kind of an off-white color, almost like the color of light produced by a house lamp. This light was in the sky next to where the star/UFO was, but the light I noticed when it flashed was quick and concentrated, not like [the] glare you might see coming from a light source. About a minute later we saw another flash in the same general area and of the same nature as before. This went on for about three minutes. All three flashes were in the same general area, [in reference] to our location. Then the flashes stopped. My mind at this point didn't know what to really make of it at the time, but I kept watching hopefully to see something else, to make some sense of it. Within a minute or two we saw a streak in the sky of the same color light as the flashes, but the streak was moving in an S-shaped pattern. I drove home that night scared out of my wits and a little excited. There was no aircraft in the area, and nothing unusual about the night except for the light.... In no way could it have been an aircraft or meteor."

CARY, January 9, 1969—Vera Matter observed a nocturnal light.

CASEYVILLE, 9 p.m., July 5, 1997—See chapter 5, "Close Encounters of the July Fourth Kind."

CENTRALIA, August 7, 1963—Nocturnal light observed.

CENTRALIA, September 9, 1970—Mrs. Arnold Gluck observed a nocturnal light.

CENTRALIA, November 24, 1970—Sam Alli and another man watched a round object travel across the night sky.

CENTRALIA, February 1971—A family experienced a close encounter of the second kind.

CENTRALIA, night of November 24, 1971—Close encounter of the second kind. See chapter 6, "Don't Look Now, but You're Being Followed."

CENTRALIA, August 17, 1978—Nocturnal light observed from North Cherry Street.

CHAMPAIGN, August 31, 1970—Robert Peterson observed a nocturnal light from Kirby Avenue.

CHAMPAIGN, October 13, 1977—Daylight disk observed.

CHAMPAIGN, 9:45 p.m., November 5, 1995—Close encounter of the second kind. See chapter 6, "Don't Look Now, but You're Being Followed."

CHANNAHON, 11:35 p.m., April 5, 1998—A young driver was chased by a triangular UFO. (For more information see chapter 4, "The 1998 UFO Wave.")

CHARLESTON, 11 p.m., May 21, 1996—Four young people camping saw a large white light and then a huge, triangular UFO with two red lights on one side. It illuminated the campsite with a "spotlight."

CHEBANSE, 9 p.m., May 12, 1998—A husband and wife each observed flying disks. (For more information see chapter 4, "The 1998 UFO Wave.")

CHERRY VALLEY, September 30, 1956—Mrs. L. L. Leonard experienced a close encounter of the second kind.

CHERRY VALLEY, September 30, 1956—A UFO was observed, and afterward "angel hair," a mysterious spiderweblike substance associated with UFOs, was found.

CISNE, August 1, 1963—See sidebar "At First Harold and I Did Not Think Much about It, Because We Were Worried about the Cow."

CHICAGO HEIGHTS, March 3, 1967—Eugene LaBelle observed a nocturnal light.

CHICAGO HEIGHTS, September 4, 1975—Nocturnal light observed.

CLINTON, August 15, 1968—College student Ralph Mollet observed a nocturnal light while driving west on U.S. Highway 54.

CLINTON, October 17, 1973—Charles Williams observed a nocturnal light.

COATSBURG, July 7, 1970—A mother and her children saw an orange nocturnal light while driving north on Highway 1.

COFFEEN, January 26, 1967—A close encounter of the first kind occurred near Highway 185.

COLUMBIA, 10:30 p.m., July 4, 1997—See chapter 5, "Close Encounters of the July Fourth Kind."

COLLINSVILLE, 10:40 p.m., March 15, 1995—A St. Louis resident, looking across the Mississippi River toward Illinois, saw a blue-green object with a luminous white tail. It flew slowly.

COLLINSVILLE, 9:40 p.m., July 4, 1997—See chapter 5, "Close Encounters of the July Fourth Kind."

COVINGTON, May 4, 1971—Herb Williams observed three nocturnal lights near Highway 177.

CRESTWOOD, December 10, 1975—Nocturnal light observed.

CRETE, 4:05 p.m., August 29, 1960—See sidebar "The Ones That Stumped Even the Air Force."

CRYSTAL LAKE, June 12, 1977—A Mr. Boega experienced a close encounter of the third kind.

DANVERS, July 1, 1970—Close encounter of the first kind.

DANVILLE, November 6, 1957—State police officers Calvin Showers and John Matulis watched for 20 minutes a brilliant white light, which changed color to amber and then to orange as they chased it. It apparently made the radio in the car fail.

DANVILLE, April 22, 1995—A 77-year-old woman saw a strange object ascend "like a jet" near the airport.

"AT FIRST HAROLD AND I DID NOT THINK MUCH ABOUT IT, BECAUSE WE WERE WORRIED ABOUT THE COW"

CISNE, August 1, 1963—Roberta Flexter wrote to the local paper to report a sighting she had made with her husband, Harold: "My husband and I were at the farmhouse watching a cow that was to have a calf. We were waiting in the field, sitting in the truck with our lights on, and I saw this light coming up from behind some trees, and it went real high in the sky and then it just hovered there. At first Harold and I did not think much about it, because we were worried about the cow.

"I would glance at it once in a while and it was still there. It looked like a great big light. We thought it might be a star, but Harold said it was too big for a star, so we watched it for about 45 minutes. In the meantime, the cow had moved, so we started the motor and was moving [sic] when the light began to move.

"I told Harold to stop and turn the lights and motor off. That light was moving real fast and did not make any noise. At least if it

did, we did not hear it. I could see the form of it as it went overhead. When I first saw it, it was a big light, and when it moved
overhead it looked like a kite-shaped object. There was a big light
on the front, and on the back was a red light, which was smaller.

"As I said, it went real fast, and after it passed overhead it
looked like the red light was closer to the big light. It faded away,
and then we had to get the vet for the cow. She had a dead calf.
The vet said it was coming too soon. We did not know what to
think of it."

The same day, according to the Mt. Vernon Register News, "unexplained lights danced in the night skies over Wayne County for
the second time this week. Authorities said residents east and
west of Fairfield reported seeing two bright lights, one described
as kite-shaped with a comet-like tail. Both lights, they said, traveled rapidly across the skies. One of them dimmed, temporarily."

In Fairfield, at 9 p.m. the next night, scores of people saw a
similar UFO. Mike Hill and Geoffrey Uphoff had a good view from
Uphoff's farm, four miles east of town.

"Mike and I were sitting in the yard talking," Uphoff said. "And
all of a sudden Mike said, 'Did you turn your porch light on? Look
at that up there. It looks like a big diamond.' I quickly saw it. It was
moving from the west, along over the railroad track to the east.
Never saw anything like it before. I ran inside and called the police
station. When I got back, Mike said, 'Look there, here comes
something else—it's a jet plane.'

"And sure enough, there was another object, but it didn't have
blinker lights like a jet. Anyway, the diamond object suddenly
swung around toward the jet plane object, and as it neared it, the
lights on the diamond object went out. After the plane passed,
there it was again. And then the light changed to a different glow,
and she swooped around towards us with lightninglike speed and
at this point looked like a kite with a long tail. Quickly it circled
back to the south and seemed to hover right there in the heavens
at about a 45-degrees [sic] angle over what would be the village
of Merriam. Finally, it disappeared down toward Grayville. It was
big and it was bright. It looked like it might be a thousand or more
feet up. It made no sound whatever."

The same night, 18-year-old Ronnie Austin claimed to have
been chased home by a big, bright object in the sky, near Keenes.

Two days later, a ball of fire "as big as a washtub" hovered over Mt. Vernon. Many reported the UFO to the police. Former mayor Harry Bishop said the light came down Central Road from the north and was "the brightest light I have ever seen. It appeared to be only about [300] or 400 feet high, was oval shaped, and was about the size of a washtub." It then flew west and disappeared "like somebody had turned the light off." The object then briefly reappeared and made a light, whirring sound. Bishop said, "I thought those people at Fairfield were crazy when I read about the strange things they have been seeing in the sky, but I've changed my mind now."

DARMSTADT, December 21-22, 1974—Four miles west of the community, Kin Lloyd and others had a close encounter of the second kind.

DAVIS JUNCTION, November 3, 1973—Nocturnal light observed.

DECATUR, July 1, 1970—Ralph Kramer experienced a close encounter of the first kind near Rea's Bridge.

DECATUR, August, 1930—Between the airship and the modern eras of UFOs, Jack Huffman saw a daylight disk.

DECATUR, July 3, 1947—Claude Price saw a nocturnal light near Highway 36.

DECATUR, July 22, 1970—Leon Worley observed a nocturnal light near Grove Road.

DECATUR, July 30, 1970—John Garren observed a nocturnal light west of town.

DECATUR, June 22, 1971—David Krause observed a nocturnal light near his home on Point Bluff Drive.

DECATUR, the night of July 1, 1971—Ralph Kramer was driving with his five children and a city firefighter, east on Highway 24. All of them felt frightened by the 30 or so red and green lights they saw, flying in formation over the tree line to their right. But while they were afraid, Kramer said, they also "felt kind of an attraction to them—possibly a mental attraction." The lights were arranged strangely, as if in the shape of an acorn. They did not blink or flash and stayed in the same positions relative to each other, leading Kramer to believe that they were attached to a frame of some sort. Suddenly the colored lights went out, replaced by three bright "searchlights" that illuminated the whole area. The UFO was within 100 feet, though no one could hear the sound of a motor. Then the white lights, too, went out, and the UFO quickly left.

DECATUR, September 7, 1971—Robert T. Dillow observed a nocturnal light.

DECATUR, September 7–18, 1971—Leonard Strum observed nocturnal lights.

DECATUR, July 11, 1972—Ralph Donovan and others saw a nocturnal light.

DECATUR, February 11, 1973—Mrs. Jack Huffman saw an oval-shaped object during the day, from Tolly's Supermarket.

DEERFIELD, April 5, 1977—a daylight disk was seen from Interstate 94.

DEERFIELD, June 10, 1977—Nocturnal light observed.

DE KALB, October 28, 1978—Clinton Jesser observed a nocturnal light.

DE KALB COUNTY, November 3, 1973—Nocturnal light observed.

DES PLAINES, October 10, 1975—A nocturnal light was observed.

DES PLAINES, November 5, 1978—A daylight disk was seen from Howard Avenue.

DOLTON, July 4, 1947—Andrew Wolfe observed a nocturnal light.

DUPO, August 21, 1969—Close encounter of the second kind.

DUPO, October 4, 1970—Russell Griffin observed a nocturnal light.

DUPO, 9 p.m., July 4, 1997—See chapter 5, "Close Encounters of the July Fourth Kind."

EAST ALTON, 9:45 p.m., July 4, 1997—See chapter 5, "Close Encounters of the July Fourth Kind."

EAST AURORA, 9 p.m., May 24, 1995—A man saw a "very bizarre" object.

EAST DUNDEE, August 9, 1975—Nocturnal light observed.

EAST PEORIA, July 7, 1947—Forrest Higginbotham observed a daylight disk.

EAST PEORIA, September 24, 1966—Ray Watts experienced a close encounter of the first kind.

EAST PEORIA, April 12, 1971—Ray Watts saw a boomerang-shaped nocturnal light.

EAST ST. LOUIS, November 5, 1957—Daylight disk observed.

EDWARDSVILLE, January 14, 1976—Nocturnal light observed.

EFFINGHAM, December 6, 1970—Mae Jannett and her family observed a nocturnal light while traveling east on Interstate 70.

ELBURN, August 19, 1959—Nocturnal light observed.

ELGIN, 1:15 a.m., October 10, 1998—"While looking up at the sky I noticed a bright light hovering above the sky. Then I noticed a jet airliner traveling in the same area, and I noticed the bright object was further away and brighter than the jet. Then the object began to shift to the east at a very slow rate. At the same time its glow was changing from bright white to somewhat of a fireball color. It changed directions several times. I took a picture of it with my digital camera while a second jet airliner was crossing the same vicinity. There were no clouds in the sky. It was sunny out. The way it changed directions was very awkward. It was very subtle but quick."

The digital photo showed the UFO only after the witness zoomed in to the image and increased the contrast.*

ELK GROVE VILLAGE, May 10, 1973—A Mr. Schmidt had a close encounter of the second kind at the Ned Brown Forest Preserve.

ELK GROVE VILLAGE, July 23, 1975—Nocturnal light observed.

ELMHURST, July 8, 1947—Peter Monte observed a nocturnal light.

ELMHURST, November 16, 1975—Nocturnal light observed.

ELMWOOD, 9:15 p.m., July 4, 1997—See chapter 5, "Close Encounters of the July Fourth Kind."

ELMWOOD PARK, November 4, 1957—Police officers Joseph Lukasek, Clifford Schau, and Daniel DeGiovanni watched a reddish object hover over a cemetery. They attempted to pursue it as it left the area, and as they neared the craft their headlights and spotlight dimmed.

ELVASTON, December 31, 1970—L. H. McGinnis saw a "flying flame" while traveling west on Highway 96.

ELWIN, February 13, 1971—Leonard Strum saw a daylight disk three miles south of the community, near Highway 51.

EVERGREEN PARK, January 9, 1972—C. H. Van Welzen saw a nocturnal light.

FAIRFIELD, August 1, 1963—See sidebar "At First Harold and I Did Not Think Much about It, Because We Were Worried about the Cow."

FAIRVIEW HEIGHTS, 9:35 p.m., July 4, 1997—See chapter 5, "Close Encounters of the July Fourth Kind."

FALL CREEK, February 11, 1969—Vi Gregory saw a daylight disk near Highway 57.

FARMINGTON, August 10, 1969—Mrs. John Belagna saw a nocturnal light south of town.

---

* Unfortunately, thanks to computer technology, UFO photos these days are of little value, especially when taken with digital cameras. Would-be UFO observers would do best to arm themselves with high-quality cameras with conventional film, *and* a disposable stereoscopic camera, and a motion picture camera, of course—not video, which has extremely poor resolution. The photographer should not develop the film himself or herself but turn it over to a reputable private UFO group or media outlet, on the understanding that the negatives and/or film will be returned. (The Air Force used to collect such evidence. Today no such governmental agency is officially interested. And even then, photos and film had a habit of "disappearing," so if you must use mail, make sure it's certified and insured.) And remember that no one can make you turn over the film or photos if you don't want to; for a time, bogus Air Force personnel bullied witnesses for their negatives. The Air Force had to alert all its bases of these charlatans, today nicknamed "the Men in Black"; and they weren't the friendly guys from the film or animated TV show, either.

FLANAGAN, March 8, 1967—A Mr. Kennedy observed a nocturnal light near U.S. Highway 51.

FOX RIVER GROVE, January 9, 1969—Nocturnal light observed.

FRANKLIN PARK, 10:43 p.m., July 11, 1998—A perfect sphere was observed. (For more information see chapter 4, "The 1998 UFO Wave.")

FREEBURG, January 19, 1968—Nocturnal light observed by Phil Nichols and others.

FREEBURG, August 13, 1971—Beaulah Wilderman observed a nocturnal light.

FREEBURG, 10:45 p.m., July 4, 1997—See chapter 5, "Close Encounters of the July Fourth Kind."

FREEPORT, July 6, 1947—Elmer H. Schirmer observed a daylight disk.

FREEPORT, November 8, 1967—Harvey Toepfer observed a nocturnal light.

FULTS, 11:30 p.m., July 12, 1997—Here's a very odd sighting, or a hoax. Two people saw a red glowing rectangle with a bright light on its left end and a less bright light on its right end, which pulsed rhythmically to "booming sounds" that the object gave off. The two left to get a camera, but the object was gone when they returned. They did, however, find a purple rubber ball with a hole burned through it. The next day the ball was gone, and in its place the two found some sticks arranged to spell out "DELGOU." The many dramatic elements in this event make it, in my mind, difficult to credit.

GALENA, February 13, 1969—Nocturnal light observed.

GALESBURG and **MOLINE**, March 6, 1967—Deputy Sheriff Frank Courson saw an object shaped somewhat like the rubber cup one would see under a furniture leg. On top of the object was a dome. The lower portion rotated rapidly, and its rim pulsated with red light. It approached the officer and passed low over him, making a hissing sound.

GALESBURG, ca. March 9, 1967—Two housewives saw a pancake-shaped object with a rounded top. It pulsed with a red glow and had red lights around its edge. The object approached the women and then let loose with a flash of bright white light that lasted 10 seconds. It then flew to the north and disappeared from view.

GALVA, August 1972—R. E. Royce experienced a close encounter of the second kind.

GERMANTOWN, May 14, 1972—Janice Schwaegel observed a daylight disk.

GLASGOW, July 7, 1947—J. C. Star observed a daylight disk.

GLEN ELLYN, 8 p.m., July 1, 1963—See sidebar "The Ones That Stumped Even the Air Force."

GLENVIEW, July 4, 1975—Close encounter of the first kind.

GLENVIEW, July 21, 1977—Nocturnal light observed.

GLENVIEW, 9:30 p.m., April 18, 1998—A group of young people observed a triangular UFO. (For more information see chapter 4, "The 1998 UFO Wave.")

GODFREY, November 1965—Bob Hewitt observed a nocturnal light.

GODFREY, August 9, 1970—Duane Springman observed a nocturnal light.

GODFREY, 6:15 p.m., October 15, 1995—A man and his two sons saw what appeared to be the moon. It was the same size and color as the moon, but it was sort of hazy and moved. They pursued it in their car. Finally, the object "winked out."

GRAND TOWER, March 1956—C. B. Clark observed a nocturnal light.

GRAND TOWER, March 22, 1973—Oscar Wills and other public service company employees saw a UFO over a power station.

GRANITE CITY, 5:45 p.m., August 1, 1996—Two people saw a "pulsating ball" from their yard. "We noticed what we thought was a sky-writer plane, but as we watched it changed into a glowing blue ball that as it pulsed, it got bigger. It was in the western sky and we were gauging its movements by the electric wires. It moved erratically." As the object swung to its most extreme position, it turned pink, started getting smaller, and finally disappeared high in the sky.

GRANITE CITY, 9 and 9:15 p.m., July 4, 1997—See chapter 5, "Close Encounters of the July Fourth Kind."

GRAPE CREEK, 2:30 a.m., April 25, 1995—Two youths saw a flash in the sky and then a "vapor trail" streaking downward. In the woods nearby they then saw an intense green, strobing light.

HAMILTON, December 31, 1968—Gary Hanson observed a nocturnal light.

HAMILTON, August 29, 1969—Ken Thomas and another boy had a close encounter of the second kind.

HAMILTON, January 21, 1971—Raymond Todd observed a nocturnal light.

HAYWORTH, 9 p.m., August 19, 1995—A man saw four strange lights in the sky. They reappeared the next night.

HENRY COUNTY, March 10, 1963—See entry for Knox County, same date.

HERALD, August 1960—Nella-Jo Newcomb observed a nocturnal light.

HERRIN, October 12, 1967—Nocturnal light observed.

HIGHLAND, October 28, 1973—Don Taylor experienced a close encounter of the second kind.

HILLSIDE, June 21, 1963—Janice McKay experienced a close encounter of the second kind.

HODGKINS, 9:15 p.m., September 15, 1998—"I had just gotten to work and had time to spare to sit. It was dark. The parking lot lights had not come on yet, so the sky was pretty clear. There were no clouds, and it was a perfect evening. I had glanced around a bit and was going to grab my book when I saw a plane in the sky that looked like either a medium-size prop plane or a private jet. Behind this plane, about 50 to 100 feet or so, was a glowing red ball. The plane could not be that long for the altitude it was flying at. Behind the glowing red ball was what looked to be three helicopters in formation. I was able to tell they were helicopters because the lights on the tail [of each helicopter] were flickering from the tail rotor. They flew from east to west until they disappeared over the treetops. I tried in earnest to find someone to witness what I had just seen, but again I was early and no one was around to see it in time."

HODGKINS, 10:30 p.m., December 29, 1998—"Several coworkers and I were at work by the quarry in Hodgkins and saw something in the sky. It was a clear night, just a couple days after Christmas, and the area we were in was located around forest preserves and [had] low lighting. We looked up toward the north end of the sky because there were several lights in the distance. Everyone kept saying they were planes but then quickly dismissed that idea when the lights began to change from white to blue to red, in very short bursts, so fast that the colors seemed to blend together. These lights were stationary in their positions. There were five of them: three formed a perfect triangle and the other two just stayed outside of the triangle. They never moved for five minutes, and then all of a sudden one would disappear completely and reappear on the other side of the triangle. This pattern repeated itself several times, but the triangle always stayed constant and the lights kept flickering colors. We didn't stay outside long because we had to work and also because no one believed it could be a UFO—maybe [it was] just something that was happening over Lake Michigan with helicopters or something. Helicopters don't flash several colors at an amazing speed, stay stationary for a while, and disappear completely and reappear."

HOFFMAN, March 13, 1971—Nocturnal light observed.

HOFFMAN ESTATES, 8:51 a.m., November 26, 1998—"I was driving east on Illinois 58 in Hoffman Estates. I came to a stop at an intersection when I happen to look up in the air. At that exact moment, a green streak went from the west to the east, high in the air, and then made a sharp 90-degree turn to the south, and then disappeared. I had two other passengers in the car, and neither one of them saw the event. I pulled into a parking lot to get out and keep looking and did not see anything except regular airplanes in the sky. I know those were airplanes since being within 10 miles of Chicago's O'Hare Airport."

HOMEWOOD, March 3, 1967—Nocturnal light observed.

HOOPESTON, November 14, 1975—Nocturnal light observed.

HOYLETON, December 17, 1975—Nocturnal light observed.

HUEY, August 15, 1967—Nocturnal light observed.

HUNTLEY, March 2, 1955—Close encounter of the first kind.

HUNTSVILLE, October 15, 1975—Nocturnal light observed.

ITASCA, March 8, 1969—Near Highway 53, Raymond Richards observed a nocturnal light.

JACKSONVILLE, October 5, 1971—John Irlam observed a nocturnal light.

JACKSONVILLE, 9:30 a.m., October 18, 1998—While stopped on a country road, four people saw an orangish light appear out of nowhere. It traveled slowly south until it passed out of sight. About 10 minutes later another light appeared in the same spot from which the first had come. Eventually, seven more lights appeared in the same way, at 10-minute intervals. Bizarre!

JERSEYVILLE, July 22, 1963—A UFO was seen in the morning and late afternoon. The later sighting was made by Police Sergeant Kenneth Weller and officer Howard Sandberg while on patrol at 4:30 p.m. They returned to headquarters for binoculars so they could get a better look. The object resembled a spinning disk with a black central body, rimmed with lights. Ladderlike attachments were seen descending from the craft. At intervals the UFO moved up and

WHY DON'T SCIENTISTS SEE THEM?

The short answer is: they do. Here's an excellent report made by a geophysicist.

IPAVA, 9:15 p.m., October 1, 1998—"We were moving harvesting equipment from a remote field back to the farm. While driving, I had observed two orange fireballs in the southern [quarter of the sky] and two in the western quarter of the sky. A cold front had passed through earlier, and viewing conditions were optimal.

"The fireballs were distinctly orange, had a definite round shape, did not move, were all of the same apparent size, and faded quickly after about four seconds. There was no pattern to their appearance. Two were seen at the same time to the west. I could see only a small area of the sky while driving but saw these while driving, for only 15 minutes. The fireballs were approximately the size of the full moon, about half a degree of arc.

"After arriving at the farm on the prairie at 9:15 p.m., I asked the other drivers if they had seen the fireballs, but no one had. We scanned the sky and noticed a very bright light to the southwest, low to the horizon. It was a point source [of light] but did not appear to be moving. I determined that it was not a planet because it was south of the plane of the ecliptic [most of the planets, especially those visible to the naked eye, tend to orbit in the same plane, called by astronomers 'the plane of the ecliptic'].

"We observed it for a while, until we realized it was gaining altitude. It soon resembled car headlights about two miles away and was at about 15 degrees elevation. At this point it became evident that it was an object moving directly at us and maintaining altitude. I remembered I had my Pentax [camera] with a 205-millimeter lens in my truck and started taking pictures. The film was ASA 200 and did not turn out.

"The object flew almost directly over our heads. It had three bright, white lights that were visible from all angles. There was a white light on each side, with the center light slightly ahead of the other two. There was also a cluster of green lights in the center of the object, with one or two red ones intermixed. These lights were very faint and did not blink. There was no sound whatsoever.

"As it continued to the northeast, the white lights were still dominant, but there was also faint reddish lights visible from behind. We eventually became bored with the event and left the property about 9:30 p.m., with the object still visible above the horizon. We were treated to two more orange fireballs in the west as we left. My cousin says he returned to the field at 10 p.m. and saw the object again.

"I recall an incident in April of this year just a few miles to the north of this sighting, that I saw the same lights [the rear aspect] at about 10 p.m., along the same flight path as observed on October 1. I had lost sight of them as they moved behind a neighborhood house.

"I am a 40-year-old geophysicist, and my cousin is a 43-year-old farmer. His 12-year-old son and my 16-year-old nephew were the other witnesses. My nephew reported that someone at school claimed to have seen an object in a field near Vermont, Illinois, that night. That would have been about five miles to the southwest of us and consistent with our sighting."

down, east and west, and north and south. It was also seen by others traveling home from work. Nearby Scott Air Force Base denied responsibility for the object.

JERSEYVILLE, 6:25 a.m., December 9, 1998—"I was driving south on Route 267 this morning at sunrise, when I noticed a light to the right side of the highway. It was the only object in the sky in that direction and appeared to be the brightness of a planet. However, it moved west to east. It was about to cross the plane of the highway when I looked down to the radio for the time. At that point, I looked up and it had disappeared. There was no remnant. No flashing light. Nothing. The sun was not up, only an orange band in the east."

(It is possible for planets to appear motionless and even move west to east in the sky. In fact, it is this retrograde motion that gave the ancients the knowledge that these lights in the sky were not just ordinary stars. I wish I knew how long this sighting lasted. If the witness actually perceived the object to be moving, it is unlikely to have been a planet.)

JOLIET, June 24, 1947—Charles Kastle saw a daylight disk 10 miles east of the city.

JOLIET, May 17, 1954—Daylight disk observed.

JOLIET, August 5, 1977—Daylight disk observed.

JOLIET, 9 p.m., December 10, 1995—A man saw a bright red streak of light traveling from west to east. There were many similar reports the night before, some by Illinois state police; see the listing for Springfield, December 9, 1995.

JOLIET, 3:20 p.m., December 19, 1995—While driving east on U.S. Highway 30, an observer well versed in astronomy and weather saw two objects in a clear sky, hovering. One object appeared to "float" around the other. They were colored dull aluminum on top and black on the bottom. Both the tops and bottoms of the objects were less than perfect circles. The objects were observed for about 8 miles of travel.

JOPPA, March 23, 1966—Nocturnal light observed.

KAMPSVILLE, November 1974—Janice Ewen observed a daylight disk.

KANKAKEE, November 1954—Close encounter of the second kind.

KANKAKEE, January 27, 1964—Earle Applegate experienced a close encounter of the first kind.

KANKAKEE, October 12, 1970—Ronald Scrogham experienced a close encounter of the first kind.

KARNAK, 8 p.m., December 13, 1996—"There were two ships moving at high speeds. One was shaped like a pencil, and the other was shaped like a submarine with wings. They were both a shining gray. I was sitting outside, staring at the stars, when I saw a streak of green light, followed by an explosion. Right before the explosion I saw what seemed to be [the] bigger ship, shaped like a pencil, shooting something blue at the ship that exploded."

KEENES, August 2, 1963—See the sidebar "At First Harold and I Did Not Think Much about It, Because We Were Worried about the Cow."

KEYESPORT, January 1, 1975—Debbie Jannett had a close encounter of the second kind on Mulberry-Keyesport Road.

KINDERHOOK, February 19, 1972—Mrs. Michael Murphy observed a nocturnal light.

KINMUNDY, April 14, 1972—William Arlen observed a nocturnal light.

KNOX COUNTY, March 10, 1964—Scores of people in Knox and Henry Counties saw a very odd UFO. Knox County Deputy Sheriff Fran Courson said it was "very distinguishable." It was about 35 feet in diameter and had flashing red, white, and amber lights. He and others watched through binoculars for more than an hour and a half as the object hovered over two transmission towers and was eventually joined by a second craft. "It was bluish white and pulsating red," Courson said, and had "a rim that looked like it was about five feet thick." He described it as shaped like an overturned bowl. Others, groping for a label, heard the UFO make a roaring sound and dubbed it a "giant vacuum cleaner."

LA HARPE, 8:15 a.m., January 5, 1966—Close encounter of the third kind. See chapter 6, "Don't Look Now, but You're Being Followed."

LAKE ZURICH, May 12, 1969—Greg Lucht experienced a close encounter of the first kind at the intersection of Highway 53 and Dundee Road.

LAWRENCEVILLE, June 8, 1964—Helen Reed experienced a close encounter of the first kind two and a half miles west of town, on U.S. Highway 50.

LEMONT, 7:42 a.m., April 2, 1999—A 41-year-old nurse and her 16-year-old daughter, an honors student ranked second in her class, saw a UFO in the shape of an equilateral triangle. Along each edge were white and blue lights, and at each corner was a white light. "My daughter actually drove under the object," the woman said. On the bottom of the craft were concave lines and a central red light. The object appeared to be floating low in the sky. Eventually it flew away, with one of its straight edges to the front rather than one of its corners. "Neither one of us has ever seen anything like this before!" the nurse said.

LENZBURG, 8:30 p.m., July 4, 1997—See chapter 5, "Close Encounters of the July Fourth Kind."

LEWISTOWN, July 19, 1971—Robert Geger observed a nocturnal light.

LIBERTY, October 5, 1971—Lyle Ferguson observed a nocturnal light.

LIBERTYVILLE, probably around 9 p.m., year unknown; 1960s?—"I was a young boy, perhaps 12 or so. My friends and I were playing in the street, a game that we called Frisbee football. Anyway, I was in their end zone and threw a pass all the way down the street, and all the kids took off running, [saying] 'Save me!' I looked over my right shoulder and saw a bright green sphere hovering about, which illuminated the surrounding area."

LINCOLNSHIRE, June 30, 1975—Close encounter of the first kind.

LINCOLNSHIRE, 4:45 a.m., December 10, 1998—A fireball was observed traveling south to north. Its tail was four to five times larger than the object itself. After seven seconds, it disappeared.

LINDENDALE PARK, January 4, 1975—Nocturnal light observed.

LITCHFIELD, April 1970—From a drive-in, Jerrel Carner observed a nocturnal light.

LITTLETON, 4:45 a.m., July 20, 1964—J. J. Winkle saw a round-topped, flat-bottomed object with a long flame shooting downward. The curved part described an arc of only 60 degrees. The flame resembled that of an acetylene torch. The object flew straight and level, made a half-loop, and then ascended. The sighting lasted about a minute.

LOCKPORT, May 1912—Between the airship and modern UFO eras, Carl Howe observed a nocturnal light.

LOMBARD, August 11, 1972—Close encounter of the first kind.

LONDON MILLS, December 14, 1978—Ralph Brashear observed a nocturnal light.

LONG GROVE, March 9, 1977—Nocturnal light observed.

LONG POINT, October 9, 1960—Jack L. Sanford saw a daylight disk.

LORAINE, October 14, 1972—Edward Hagerbaumer observed a nocturnal light.

MAHOMET, December 19, 1967—on U.S. Highway 150, Maryellen Kelly experienced a close encounter of the second kind.

MANITO, 9:30 p.m., May 6, 1998—Two UFOs, "far too complex for a plane," were sighted; they were seen again at 1:26 a.m. on May 7. (For more information see chapter 4, "The 1998 UFO Wave.")

TALKING WITH ALIENS: JANUARY 23, 1999

Let's call him Steve:

"I work midnights, and this was my normal day off. I usually try to stay up most of the nights I'm off, since it's easier on the body. The dogs started to act funny. This was about 4 a.m. Central. I thought they wanted to go out, so I headed to the back door.

"I live a couple of miles from a midsize city an hour south of Chicago on Interstate 57. Our subdivision is built in a large U shape with a farm field in the center. The houses opposite mine are about 300 yards away, across the field to the east. The field is about 600 or 700 yards, north to south.

"We have had a very dense fog for the last few days due to little wind, a very deep snow cover, and temperatures in the mid-to-upper 40s. The fog had been so thick that I could not see the houses across the field behind me. Visibility has probably been 100 yards or less.

"As I approached the back door to let the dogs out, I saw a green light coming from the back yard, actually from the field behind the yard. This puzzled me since the fog was still outside. I could see it out of the window in the front of the house from the room where my computer is located. I grabbed a flashlight that was on a table and headed out. What I saw amazed me.

"I opened the door and there it was: a large object probably 40 or 50 feet off the ground. The center of the object, which had a small, intense green light on the bottom, was located about 75 or 80 yards directly behind my yard in a line with a point 5 feet to the north of my back door connecting the electrical box at the edge of the property. It was about 100 feet in diameter, since it looked like it would touch the ground if it were turned 90 degrees and extend about the same distance upward from its midpoint. It looked cigar shaped but had pointlike extensions, kind of like a Star of David but eight of them equidistant around the circumference.

"I poked my head back into the house to look for a camera. My wife took up 'scrap-booking' a few months ago and usually has a camera with film in it in the kitchen. I found the camera but no film. I was going to grab the video camera but it was in a different room. What I did see to grab was my laser pointer from my briefcase on the island in the kitchen.

"I kept the dogs inside and headed out to see this thing with my light and my laser pointer in hand. I only had a pair of slippers on but didn't think much of it till later. I shined the flashlight at the object, but the fog made it a big blur, for lack for a better word. I left it on the deck as I headed out to the edge of the yard.

"When I reached the edge of the yard and the end of the grass I stopped. I was still 70 or so yards away from the edge of it. It did not move. I shined the pointer at the object then and could see my beam and the point hit the object's belly. I then shined it on the neighbors' house[s] to get some idea how far it would go and still be visible in the fog. I could see it as far as two houses away but could not see where I knew the third house to be. So the visibility limit for the point was probably somewhere between 100 and 150 yards or so.

"I then shined the pointer on the object, running it across the bottom, making sure to run it along all the edges to better judge its size. After a few minutes of this, the light on the bottom of the object flashed once. It increased by at least, I'm guessing, three orders of magnitude. Then it went back to its previous brightness. The flash lasted maybe a quarter-second and reminded me of a photo flash, but green in color. After a few seconds it flashed again, but twice this time, each flash about half a second apart. It did it again a few seconds later, and this time it did three flashes, then a few seconds without a flash, then 5 flashes for a period of seconds, then 7 flashes.

"It was then it dawned on me these were prime numbers. I still had the pointer, and I shined 11 flashes at the green light, then 13. The object then flashed 17 at me. We were communicating.

"Then it stopped for almost a minute. At this point it's easier to just write in the number sequence of flashes. I have no idea what they mean: 19, 7, 8, 18, 19, 6, 16, 19, 21, 11, 21, 12, 13, 20, 23, 21, 24, 8.*

"After the last grouping, the light went dull, maybe a magnitude or so dimmer than it was initially. Then at the tips of the star-like projections, green lights—but a darker green or a little toward blue—came on. The object started to lift up then, moving a few feet a second at first, then moving faster. There was no sound. It looked to be going straight up. I shined the pointer on it until I could not see the point any longer but could still make out the eight lights from the projections for a few more seconds. Then it was just gone.

"The whole event took maybe 10 or 12 minutes.... Then I went out to the field to the point that was under the center of the object. The snow in the field was kind of spotty, but a circular pattern could be seen at the point I figured to be under the green light. The pattern was...a bit bigger, I think, than what I had thought the object was. My step count was 115 from my army days: this put the diameter of the circle on the ground at about 127 feet.

"I would rather not attach my name, as I think people may find out about this and think I'm crazy."

---

* Prime numbers are significant, of course, because they are divisible only by themselves and one. The full message contains numbers other than prime. For those suspecting a simple number-letter substitution code, with 1 for A, 2 for B, and so on, I've saved you the trouble. The message spells: ABCEGSGRSFPSUKULMTWUXH. The only comprehensible information I see here is "egs" and "suk," which may or may not be true. We'll have to dig a little deeper.

MANITO, 9 p.m., April 25, 1998—Three friends saw a light, which then broke into two disks, then into three. (For more information see chapter 4, "The 1998 UFO Wave.")

MARION, January 1, 1958—Construction workers watched as seven UFOs slowly passed overhead. They were all in a line, and some seemed to pulsate.

MARKHAM, January 26, 1971—Helen Swanson observed a daylight disk, a pink-and-yellow circle.

MARTINSVILLE, July 1968—James Lee observed a nocturnal light.

MASCOUTAH, May 3, 1971—On Highway 177 Herb Williams observed three nocturnal lights.

MATTOON, June 26, 1966—Jim Waltrip observed a nocturnal light.

MATTOON, September 7, 1970—Mrs. James Turner experienced a close encounter of the first kind.

MAYWOOD, October 30, 1975—Close encounter of the first kind.

MCHENRY, October 12, 1975—Nocturnal light observed.

MEREDOSIA, November 7, 1971—While traveling east on Highway 104, William Cole Jr. observed a nocturnal light.

MILAN, 1956—At the Quad City airport, a nocturnal light was observed.

MILLSTADT, 9:45 p.m., July 4, 1997—See chapter 5, "Close Encounters of the July Fourth Kind."

MOKENA, September 24, 1951—Harrison E. Bailey reported a close encounter of the fourth kind.

MOLINE, March 8, 1967—Willian Fisher saw a daylight disk from 14th Street and 16th Avenue.

MOLINE, 2:30 p.m., November 20, 1998—A woman saw a brilliant flash of green light with a tail, streaking from west to east. She insisted that it was not a meteor, as she had recently seen news footage of the Leonid meteor showers, which did not appear similar to her UFO.

MONMOUTH, July 13, 1966—Nocturnal light observed.

MOUNT MORRIS, November 3, 1973—Nocturnal light observed.

MOUNT OLIVE, December 20, 1970—John Schuessler observed a nocturnal light a mile north of town on U.S. Highway 66.

MOUNT STERLING, 9 p.m., September 12, 1998—Approximately 50 moving lights were seen, all moving up and down, "like balloons on a string," from Macomb, Illinois, to Hannibal, Missouri. KHQA-TV in Quincy filmed the UFOs on one of the six consecutive nights they were visible. The Air National Guard claimed that the lights were the afterburners of their own aircraft...after previously having reported that no maneuvers had been carried out in the area. Among the sidelights of the incident was the sighting of the mysterious unmarked black helicopters, often seen before, during and after UFO sightings and cattle mutilations; who they belong to no one knows, despite investigations by the FBI and the FAA. At any rate, one witness's report of the mystery lights is as follows: "On September 12, 1998, at approximately 9:15 p.m., I witnessed one large ball of light in the northern sky at approximately 30 degrees above the horizon. This ball of light split into two balls. The second ball traveled to the west and stopped, staying parallel with the first. The second ball started moving up and down rapidly and then traveled back to join the first. As the two joined back together, they seemed to implode into nothing. This activity lasted approximately five minutes from start to finish. I shut off my car and got out to witness this event, and there was not a sound."

MOUNT STERLING, 9:02 p.m., October 1, 1998—A large orange fireball was seen just north of town. "The fireball just sat stationary at about 30 degrees above the horizon. I then turned around and proceeded to drive south on Route 99, where the lights of the town were not a factor, and my view would not be obscured. Approximately one and a half miles south of town I saw three orange fireballs to the east of me, approximately a quarter mile from my location, at about 1000 feet in altitude. These fireballs were in a triangular formation and motionless. The location of these lights was less than a quarter of a mile east of the Western Illinois Correctional Facility." After about five minutes, the objects disappeared. "I proceeded to a small blacktop road called the Wild Cat Road, to head back to town. I then noticed what appeared to be an aircraft with two white landing lights approaching from the southwest. The craft was slow moving, like an old J-3 Cub [aircraft], and made no noise. I got out of my car and watched the craft pass over me. It was small, like a fighter jet, but was totally quiet and moved so slow. As the craft passed I noticed a string of five white lights along the trailing edge, all in a line. There were no aircraft marker lights or strobes on the object."

MOUNT VERNON, August 1 and 4, 1963—See the sidebar "At First Harold and I Did Not Think Much about It, Because We Were Worried about the Cow."

MOUNT VERNON, April 30, 1969—Nocturnal light observed southeast of town.

MOUNT VERNON, May 3, 1971—Nocturnal light observed.

MOUNT VERNON, 5 a.m., June 21, 1992—"I saw what looked like a huge dome in the middle of a cornfield. I was driving down Route 15 when I noticed the craft resting on the ground. It was about 200 yards away. It had veinlike structures on the sides of it, and spotlights all the way around the base. The dome past was flashing like an electrical arc, and it appeared to me to be in distress. There was a lot of activity around the base, like spotlights moving around frantically. The car in front of me slowed down to observe it, so I passed and got away. I saw enough of the object to know I didn't want to get any closer to it."

MURPHYSBORO, November 20, 1957—A housewife saw three white oval UFOs flying in V formation.

MURPHYSBORO, November 30, 1957—Daylight disk observed.

MURPHYSBORO, 9:45 p.m., July 24, 1997—From her pool, a woman saw an iridescent green "Frisbee-like" cylinder flying south to north. She believed it was flying too low to be an airplane.

NAPERVILLE, 1:40 p.m., March 26, 1962—See sidebar "The Ones That Stumped Even the Air Force."

NASHVILLE, January 3, 1975—Mrs. Ralph Kleine observed a nocturnal light.

NASHVILLE, February 25, 1976—Close encounter of the third kind, northwest of town.

NAUVOO, November 29, 1970—Close encounter of the second kind.

NEOGA, 4:10 a.m., May 10, 1997—A delivery person for the *Journal-Gazette* was driving six miles west of town when "a craft came over a tree line on a hill just west of me. The craft made no noise, and it had hundreds of red 'dot' lights all over the bottom of it. I couldn't believe what I was seeing, and I watched it cross the bottom [of the] valley, making its way southeast. I kept watching and tried to follow it, but I had to go down the road about a half-mile before I could go east. I watched it as it crossed the bottomland. I came to a hill that I had to go up, at which time I lost sight of it. When I got to the top of the hill, I could no longer see it. I got out of the car and stood there looking in all directions but never saw it again. It just disappeared in the 30 seconds it was out of my view. It was so weird. No noise, so sudden. My mind is trying to tell me that I didn't even see it."

NEW ATHENS, June 16–17, 1973—Nocturnal lights observed.

NEW BADEN, March 21, 1967—Close encounter of the second kind, near Highway 161.

NEW BADEN, August 5, 1969—Charles J. Brandmeyer had a close encounter of the first kind while traveling east on Highway 161.

NEW DELHI, nighttime, July 2, 1956—Mrs. Horace Ash observed a cigar-shaped object.

NEWTON, October 10, 1966—Close encounter of the first kind.

NEWTON, October 14, 1966—Close encounter of the second kind.

NORMAL, summer 1964—I'm afraid that I feel this sighting is suspect, given the witness's age at the time. Was it a dream? Possibly, but then why is there no drama? "This happened when I was a kid. I was an amateur astronomy buff and spent a lot of time lying in a lawn chair in the backyard, studying the stars. One night during the summer, when I was about eight years old, I was lying in the backyard as usual, looking at the stars more or less to the north. I suddenly noticed almost directly overhead a ring of red and blue or blue-green lights, with a dark interior that blocked out the stars. There were, as I recall, six lights total, evenly spaced in a circular pattern, alternating red and blue. The object was moving very slowly, apparently from the direction I had been looking at the stars before. I had not seen it approach. It was just suddenly above me. It took what seemed like several minutes as it very slowly moved over the house. As it passed over the house, I could see reflections of the lights off of the television antenna on the roof. I estimate now, from the angles the lights would have had to reflect, that the object was probably no more than 15 to 20 feet above the roof. Assuming that is correct, then the size of it was probably about 20 to 30 feet in diameter. As it passed over the house, I ran around to the front yard to continue watching it. I had to take my eyes off it while I was running. When I got around to the front yard and looked for it again, it was gone! There was a clear view across some fields to the south, where it could have gone, but I didn't see it. Considering the speed at which I was moving, and the direction, I should have been able to see it for quite some time. It just disappeared as quickly as it came. I have no serious explanation for this incident, and it's been on my mind ever since."

NORMAL, October 27, 1975—Nocturnal light observed.

NORMAL, July 31, 1977—Daylight disk observed.

NORTHBROOK, 6:11 a.m., February 28, 1949—Ben Cole, Jr., saw a flaming object hurtle from the east and then disintegrate south of Chicago. Forty miles away, Ed Maher saw a "rocket," half a block long, speed from east to south. The tail of the object seemed to fall into pieces as the object dove into a large cloud. There was no sound.

NUTWOOD, January 17, 1969—South of town Edward Clark observed a nocturnal light.

OAK BROOK, August 11, 1972—Nocturnal light observed.

OAK BROOK, November 19, 1975—Nocturnal light observed.

OAK FOREST, August 16, 1960—Former Air Force pilot Harry Deerwester was flying when he saw a disk hover and "bobble around" in various directions.

ODIN, 1968—Ora Prahl observed a nocturnal light.

O'FALLON, August 1950—Clarence O. Dargie saw a daylight disk.

O'FALLON, October 18, 1973—Close encounter of the second kind.

OLNEY, 9:25 p.m., July 4, 1997—See chapter 5, "Close Encounters of the July Fourth Kind."

OLNEY, 8:30 p.m., January 20, 1999—While stargazing, a witness saw a dimly lit, gray V-shaped craft coming from west to east. It disappeared into the east within 10 seconds.

ORANGEVILLE, 7 p.m., February 3, 1999—See chapter 2, "'Two Beings Were Leaving My Bedroom.'"

OREGON, September 1971—Myrnie Worsely observed a nocturnal light.

OREGON, 11:49 p.m., April 21, 1995—Two young people saw a saucer-shaped object with a dome as it passed overhead. It had a red light in its "front" and a strobing red light in its "rear." A similar object was also seen the next day.

ORLAND PARK, 9:40 p.m., December 1, 1995—A man saw four to five very bright multicolored lights to the south. They appeared to move, but only slightly.

ORLAND PARK, 5:40 a.m., September 19, 1997—"When pulling out of my driveway to go to work, I turned north onto West Avenue and stopped at the stop sign. A bright white stationary light caught my eye, which I thought was an airplane against the west horizon. I remained stopped at the sign because the light was so bright. As I watched it, it appeared to stop and start very quickly several times. I pulled away from the stop sign when I saw another vehicle behind me, only to see the object speed off faster than any plane goes traveling in the same direction as my car. To view it better I decided to turn off the main road in an easterly direction, put my car in park, shut off the radio, and was putting my automatic window down when I suddenly saw an [airborne object] to the left of my car and above me. Thinking this was the bright object I had seen, it would have been necessary for it to have made a sharp 45-degree angle in order for me to have seen it so quickly. It scared me tremendously, and I remember reminding myself that there were other vehicles on the road at this time, and I must not be the only one seeing this. With my car window down I was looking out to see the bright light but instead saw an aircraft that seemed unusual, rectangular in shape, large (it would have taken four to five palm breadths to cover the length) but not wide (it would have taken one-half a palm breadth to cover the width). It was a metallic bronze-chocolate color with a narrow head and fan-shaped horizontal small tail compared to the large rectangular body. No white light was visible, and there was no sound made by the craft. It seemed to move slowly above me, taking five to six seconds to pass, and was not visible in the eastern horizon afterwards; however, the area is densely populated with homes and large trees. I was afraid it was some type of military aircraft that had gotten off course, and flying so low, I thought it would crash into the surrounding homes. Two rows of eight to twelve lights that were circular and not revolving or shining a beam were on each side of the craft. Each row was single in color and one row was red and the other blue, but I cannot remember the sequence of the color. The tail also had a row of either red or blue lights [that] were perpendicular to the craft and only five or six circular nonbeaming lights. The body of the craft was wider than the sides and angled down like a single step to the edges. The lights were beneath each edge, although I could not see the entire left edge of the craft. After it passed, I remember sitting in my car for several seconds wondering what it was and what I should do. Not wanting to be late for work, I continued east on the side street to LaGrange Road, thinking any aircraft that big and that low I would be able to see when I was past the trees and houses. However, it was nowhere to be seen. I went to work and returned home at approximately [4 p.m.] when I contacted the Federal Aviation Agency, only to be told that most of their personnel had left for the day, and they had no reports of unusual aircraft that day.

PANA, February 8, 1973—Robert Woidt saw an orange ball of light at night.

PARIS, October 9, 1951—A pilot saw a UFO shaped like an oblate spheroid, hovering. He turned his plane toward it, and the object "shot away."

PARIS, March 9, 1955—Eugene Metcalf had a close encounter of the second kind.

PARIS, July 18, 1957—Harold Mathes saw a daylight disk.

PARK RIDGE, July 17, 1975—Nocturnal light observed.

PARK RIDGE, December 9, 1978—Patty Kelly had a close encounter of the first kind.

PARK RIDGE, December 14, 1978—Collette Loll observed a nocturnal light.

PEKIN, February 19, 1969—While traveling southwest on Highway 24, Ray Watts observed a nocturnal light.

PEORIA, July 7, 1947—Harry L. Spooner saw a flying saucer; Michael Boyer saw a daylight disk.

PEORIA, May 21, 1952—Rose Murphy had a close encounter of the second kind, 10 miles from the city.

PEORIA, September 24, 1966—Close encounter of the second kind.

PEORIA, 1968—Laird S. Carter observed a nocturnal light.

PEORIA, August 1968—Nocturnal light observed.

PEORIA, October 22, 1973—Lois Hargig observed a nocturnal light.

PEORIA, February 5, 1978—A nocturnal light was observed from Bradley University.

PEORIA, August 7, 1978—A nocturnal light was observed from War Memorial Drive.

PERRY COUNTY, fall 1968—Nocturnal light observed.

PERU, June 17, 1969—Flight instructor Thomas J. Reed had a close encounter of the first kind while driving on Interstate 80.

PERU, October 12, 1975—Nocturnal light observed.

PINCKNEYVILLE, February 22, 1950—A Du Quoin pilot and his wife were flying at about 2,000 feet over Pinckneyville when they saw a UFO at 5,000 feet. They flew higher to investigate and saw a disk-shaped craft about 60 feet across and 10 feet thick. The UFO tilted into the direction it was already flying and fled at a speed much faster than the airplane's 150 miles per hour.

PLAINVILLE, November 30, 1969—Russell Ator had a most definite close encounter of the second kind. His car rose up off Highway 96 as a UFO passed overhead!

PONTIAC, March 8, 1967—Nocturnal light observed.

PROSPECT HEIGHTS, spring 1953—Close encounter of the third kind.

PROSPECT HEIGHTS, September 1975—Greg Poch observed a nocturnal light.

QUINCY, mid-January, 1971—Close encounter of the second kind. See chapter 6, "Don't Look Now, but You're Being Followed."

QUINCY, April 9, 1971—Victor Hubbard saw an object with lights in triangle formation fly through the night sky.

QUINCY, June 15, 1972—Earl F. Watts observed a nocturnal light.

QUINCY, August 29, 1972—Hilda Christison and another witness saw a fast-moving nocturnal light.

QUINCY, October 8, 1972—Nocturnal light observed.

QUINCY, September 30, 1975—Nocturnal light observed.

QUINCY, September 30, 1973—Nocturnal light observed.

RANDOLPH, May 1974—Possible landing marks found.

RANTOUL, January 9, 1956—Twenty miles southwest of the community, a nocturnal light was observed.

RED BUD, 4 p.m., April 23, 1950—Part-time photographer Dean Morgan was in the woods, looking for suitable subjects, when he happened to see a low-flying UFO. He got one good photo before the UFO flew away at "incredible" speed. The craft was a silvery domed disk, and it was hovering at tree-top level, over a clearing.

RED BUD, October 15, 1973—Robert Eicholz had a close encounter of the second kind.

REED CITY, 1923—Between the airship and modern UFO eras, Veral P. Lager observed a nocturnal light.

RINGWOOD, November 5, 1957—A luminous, round UFO followed a car to town, where it apparently caused some TV sets to dim and others to lose picture and sound, all at the same time. The UFO seemed to be at 2,000 feet and made a noise "like swishing water."

ROCK FALLS, June 15, 1968—Mary Kathleen Knowles and others saw a UFO land.

ROCKFORD, July 7, 1947—Wilbur Luckney observed a daylight disk.

ROCKFORD, April 8, 1955—John C. Gregory saw a daylight disk.

ROCKFORD, November 27, 1956—A UFO was seen by John C. Gregory and was also observed on radar.

ROCKFORD, October 1, 1967—Daylight disk observed.

ROCKFORD, 12:05 a.m., September 1, 1979—Between Rockford and Belvidere a husband and wife saw a large flying object, 1,000 to 1,500 feet in diameter, which appeared to be having difficulty. It was saucer shaped and about the size of a quarter held at arm's length, about two miles in the distance. It had "windows" that rotated around the craft from left to right. The object was observed to wobble on its axis for about five minutes. Then the "window" lights went off, leaving only a blinking white light on the top center of the object. It then flew away to the northwest. The sighting occurred just west of the Bel-ford Theater. "Most people look at us strangely when we mention it.... I just gave up trying to convince people. I guess it doesn't really matter anyway. Sooner or later everyone will see these."

ROSELLE, September 20, 1963—Richard Abel had a close encounter of the first kind.

ROUND LAKE, 1:30 a.m., January 5, 1996—A woman saw two red lights maneuvering in the sky, "mimicking each other." After a while, one light stopped and turned green. They finally disappeared, one at a time.

ROUND LAKE BEACH, 12:34 a.m., July 5, 1998—Two UFOs were observed in zigzag maneuvers. (For more information see chapter 4, "The 1998 UFO Wave.")

ST. CHARLES, 1972—Possible landing marks found.

ST. JACOB, January 1, 1975—Charles Green saw a nocturnal light near old Highway 40.

SCHAUMBURG, May 10, 1973—Fred Schmidt had a close encounter of the second kind on Schaumburg Road at Interstate 90.

SCHAUMBURG, July 4, 1978—Daylight disk observed.

SCOTT AIR FORCE BASE, midnight, April 15, 1991—An Air Force air traffic controller and two others in the control tower saw a silent triangular object with two lights in each corner, moving east to west at about 200 kilometers altitude; because of the late time, height-finding radars were not in operation, but "[i]t was my job to be able to determine such information by sight." The UFO did not appear on range-finding radars. "It appeared to be about one mile south of our position."

SEYMORE, 8 p.m., August 15, 1970—Two sets of husbands and wives saw a large metallic disk, hovering noiselessly about a half-mile away. It was shaped like two saucers placed together, the lower one inverted, with another, smaller inverted saucer on top. It was at least 200 feet in diameter, and it was colored silver. No seams or antennae were visible. There were, however, bright white "jets" coming from irregularly spaced openings around the outer edge of the object. The UFO made rapid right-angle turns as the party followed in their car for 50 miles. As the craft traveled, it gained altitude, changed to an orange color and began leaving a contrail, much as a jet aircraft does. The UFO also appeared to rotate clockwise. The four people reported the sighting to Chanute Air Force Base.

SHABBONA, November 28, 1974—Pilot Hugo Feugen found his aircraft's compass to be affected in a close encounter of the second kind.

SKOKIE, November 26, 1957—James Chapman saw a nocturnal light near Skokie Highway.

SOUTH BELOIT, midnight, May 15, 1998—A "star" ascended at great speed. (For more information see chapter 4, "The 1998 UFO Wave.")

SOUTH CHICAGO HEIGHTS, July 17, 1975—Nocturnal light observed.

SOUTH HOLLAND, 10:12 p.m., May 11, 1998—A retired state police officer and a nurse observed four flying disks. (For more information see chapter 4, "The 1998 UFO Wave.")

SPARTA, February 13, 1978—Steve Patton observed a nocturnal light.

SPRINGFIELD, July 3, 1947—West of town, George Mayfield observed a nocturnal light.

SPRINGFIELD, July 8, 1947—William Bender saw a daylight disk near Washington Street; that night, John C. Burs observed a nocturnal light. The next night Marvil Wright observed a nocturnal light from the intersection of South McArthur Boulevard and Outer Park Drive.

SPRINGFIELD, July 29, 1950—Jim Graham, head pilot for the city's Capital Aviation Company, reported that an object that looked like a blue streak, trailing a reddish flame, had struck his airplane's propeller. It was the brightest light he had ever seen. There was no damage and no sound. Four others on the ground witnessed a similar UFO.

SPRINGFIELD, 7:50 p.m., July 20, 1963—A shiny silver object was seen at a high altitude. It moved back and forth but stayed in the same general area. At dusk, the UFO was no more than a point of light, which finally sped into the distance.

SPRINGFIELD, October 5, 1971—John Wells observed a nocturnal light.

SPRINGFIELD, 6:30 a.m., December 9, 1995—Illinois State Police and the Morgan County Sheriff received multiple reports from the public of bright white and blue flashes of light in the sky. The state troopers also saw the lights themselves.

STOCKTON, August 22, 1978—Dennis Jagodzinski observed a nocturnal light near the intersection of Highway 78 and U.S. Highway 20.

STREATOR, April 25, 1976—Nocturnal light observed.

SUMNER, December 2, 1996—A mother and her two daughters saw two large, white lights in the sky. The lights were surrounded by smaller white and blue lights.

SYCAMORE, 2 p.m., November 23, 1998—"As I was taking out the garbage, I noticed something moving across the night sky at a very fast rate of speed. I saw two triangle shapes, dim red in color, in formation (side by side with one of the objects just ahead of the other), moving at a high rate of speed in a southerly direction. I heard no sound. They were headed south. I'm a star watcher and always observant of the sky. It was nothing I have ever seen before, so I know [that] what I saw was not a plane or a shooting star. I observed them for about 5 seconds, then they were out of my sight. About a month ago I saw something very similar to this but did not report it. The weird thing about it is, it took place about the same time and [it took the] exact same path, but only one was observed that time, moving twice as fast.... Believe me, what I saw was no type of airliner or shooting star. It was definitely some type of unidentified flying object. I'm no expert on UFOs, but what I saw was not of this world."

TAMAROA, November 14, 1957—John Riead experienced a close encounter of the second kind on U.S. Highway 1. A very bright, circular object was observed. It hovered, made sputtering or explosive sounds, and gave off three flashes of light. Electrical power in the area failed.

TEXICO, 9:30 p.m., April 14, 1998—A triangular UFO chased a family home. (For more information see chapter 4, "The 1998 UFO Wave.")

TINLEY PARK, 11:35 p.m., August 4, 1965—See the sidebar "The Ones That Stumped Even the Air Force."

TINLEY PARK, 8:30 p.m., October 31, 1971—An anonymous caller to the National UFO Reporting Center said, "It was one evening around Halloween when I was out taking a walk in the Brementowne Estates neighborhood, where we lived at the time. I was coming toward the pool when I noticed three lights above the pool that didn't look familiar to me. I figured that when I got closer I would be able to see what they were. As I kept getting closer, they started moving off to the right. I noticed that there were a lot of dogs barking very wildly at this time. As [the object] went off to the right it also began coming in my direction. At this point, all I saw were three lights, because it was so dark out. I started to walk into a field off to my right in order to get closer to it, and it began to [come] toward me. It was very low in the sky, and I could see it lean toward me. I was no more than about 200 feet from it. As it leaned toward me, I could see a disk silhouette around it. I then got scared and stopped in my tracks. It then slowly went back away from me and floated out of sight."

TINLEY PARK, 2 a.m., July 20, 1998—Nocturnal light observed. (For more information see chapter 4, "The 1998 UFO Wave.")

TRIVOLI, February 26, 1966—Close encounter of the second kind.

URBANA, November 6, 1957—Nocturnal light observed.

VALMEYER, 10 p.m., July 4, 1997—See chapter 5, "Close Encounters of the July Fourth Kind."

VERMILION RIVER, May 9, 1971—A black cone-shaped object was photographed over an observatory.

VILLA PARK, January 15, 1968—Lori Achzehner experienced a close encounter of the second kind.

VILLA PARK, March 28, 1976—Close encounter of the first kind.

WALSH, October 5, 1971—A Mr. Stevens turned on the yard lights at his dairy farm and went to get some feed from his silo. He looked up and saw a circle of light with a red, fuzzy "neon" look, with a fog around it. It was about 25 or 30 feet above a tree, which itself measured 75 feet. It had the apparent size of a volleyball held at arm's length. From the UFO, intersecting its circle from top right to bottom left, was a beam of light, like that of a searchlight, except that it seemed to fall like a curtain onto the barnyard. After just a few minutes, a third beam of light focused on Stevens for about three seconds, placing him in a round circle of light about four feet in diameter. The UFO slowly faded away. No sound was heard during the event. Afterward, five cows were found outside their pen, which was strung with three strands of electric fencing. How they got there no one was able to understand.

WARRENVILLE, 10 p.m., August 11, 1963—See the sidebar "The Ones That Stumped Even the Air Force."

WARSAW, July 19, 1971—Nocturnal light observed.

WAUKEGAN, July 6, 1955—Ron Castator experienced a close encounter of the second kind at Beach State Park.

WAUKEGAN, May 19, 1963—R. Dean Johnson experienced a close encounter of the first kind.

THE ONES THAT STUMPED EVEN THE AIR FORCE

While the Air Force for many years accepted UFO reports, its Projects Sign, Grudge, and Blue Book worked hard to come up with explanations; some, even the projects' own personnel, said they often worked too hard, coming up with theories that were as far-fetched as aliens. (My favorite is the story of the Kentucky-based military pilot who crashed while chasing what he thought was a flying saucer. The Air Force said he'd been chasing Venus—even though astronomers pointed out that not only was Venus not visible in the Kentucky sky at that time, it wasn't even visible in the western hemisphere.)

So for a UFO report to survive Air Force scrutiny, it had to be really puzzling. Illinois has a large crop of these Air Force "unknowns":

CHICAGO, 8:30 p.m., June 25, 1952—See chapter 1, "Chicago, City of the Big...Saucers."

CHICAGO, 5:45 p.m., June 29, 1952—See chapter 1, "Chicago, City of the Big...Saucers."

CHICAGO, 11:50 p.m. July 3, 1952—See chapter 1, "Chicago, City of the Big...Saucers."

CHICAGO, 3 a.m., September 2, 1952—See chapter 1, "Chicago, City of the Big...Saucers."

CHICAGO, 4:30 p.m., April 8, 1954—See chapter 1, "Chicago, City of the Big...Saucers."

SIXTY MILES EAST OF ST. LOUIS, 5:30 p.m., November 1, 1956—Air Force Captain W. M. Lyons, an aerial weather reconnaissance officer who was also an Intelligence Division chief, was flying a T-33 jet trainer. He watched for two minutes as an orange light with a blue tinge flew across the sky.

CRETE, 4:05 p.m., August 29, 1960—Farmer Ed Schneeweis watched a shiny, round silver object fly straight up, very fast, for 18 seconds.

NAPERVILLE, 11:40 p.m., March 26, 1962—Mrs. D. Wheeler and Claudine Milligan saw six or eight red "balls," arranged in a rectangular formation, become two objects with lights. The sighting lasted 15 minutes.

GLEN ELLYN, 8 p.m., July 1, 1963—R. B. Stiles II, using a theodolite—a telescope outfitted with an instrument to measure arc—observed a light that flashed and moved around the sky. He viewed the object for about an hour and a half but sadly neglected to report any of the measurements he may have made, which could have been used to estimate the object's angular velocity and possible altitude. The object was the apparent size of a match held at arm's length, and it flashed and moved around the sky for an hour and a half.

WARRENVILLE, 10 p.m., August 11, 1963—R. M. Boersma watched a light move around the sky for 20 seconds.

CHICAGO, 10:20 p.m., May 9, 1964—See chapter 1, "Chicago, City of the Big...Saucers."

LITTLETON, 4:45 a.m., July 20, 1964—J. J. Winkle watched a 60-foot-diameter round-topped, flat-bottomed object with a long acetylene-colored flame shooting downward. It flew straight and level, made a half-loop, and then rose up. The sighting lasted one minute.

TINLEY PARK, 11:35 p.m., August 4, 1965—Two 14-year-olds watched a light move around the sky for 16 to 17 seconds.

GALESBURG and MOLINE, 4:25 a.m., March 6, 1967—Deputy Sheriff Frank Courson saw an object shaped like a rubber cup under a furniture leg. It had a dome. The bottom of the object spun rapidly, and its rim pulsated red. It approached the witness and passed overhead at low altitude, making a hissing sound.

GALESBURG, 7:10 p.m., March 9, 1967—Two housewives saw an object shaped like a pancake with a rounded top. It was pulsating red, with red lights around its rim. It approached the witnesses and seemed to explode with a brilliant white light that lasted 10 seconds and almost blinded them. Then it accelerated to the north and disappeared.

WAUKEGAN, January 3, 1967—Frank Waters observed a nocturnal light.

WAUKEGAN, April 7, 1976—Nocturnal light observed.

WAVERLY, October 17, 1973—Nocturnal light observed.

WAYNE CITY, September 21, 1971—Kimmy Gammon experienced a close encounter of the first kind at Starvation Corner.

WAYNE COUNTY, August 4, 1963—See chapter 6, "Don't Look Now, but You're Being Followed."

WEST CHICAGO, 12:30 a.m., May 15, 1995—A woman saw a round, shiny object in the sky. It hovered, then started moving, and then "just disappeared."

WEST CHICAGO, 9 p.m., June 12, 1998—This witness provides my all-time favorite UFO description: "My girlfriend and I were standing in my driveway, looking up at the moon, when she pointed out the object. It had no lights at all and moved without any sound. It was just a big, black object that was heading south, about 100 feet in the air, at a slow, steady pace. It was a bright night, so the object was silhouetted in the sky. It was very boxy in overall appearance, but not completely. Its structure was similar to that of a plane, if you cut off the tail fin and then crashed it through a spilt-level house. The object continued heading south until it disappeared beyond the tree line."

WESTERN SPRINGS, 8:04 p.m., November 6, 1957—A brilliant orange UFO with a corona was seen moving south. It then turned east, accelerating and leaving a short trail, disappearing from sight.

WEST FRANKFORT, 1927—Between the airship and modern UFO eras, a child was spanked for reporting a close encounter of the first kind, probably in March.

WESTMONT, August 1926—Frank Tezky observed a daylight disk between the airship and modern UFO eras.

WHEATON, September 29, 1958—Close encounter of the first kind.

WHEATON, August 29, 1972—Ted Vratry observed a daylight disk near the courthouse.

WHEATON, August 9, 1977—Daylight disk observed.

WHEELING, June 30, 1975—Patricia Parhad experienced a close encounter of the first kind on River Road.

WHITE OAK, January 1, 1975—Frank M. Brown observed a nocturnal light.

WINFIELD, June 9, 1961—Barry Stark observed a nocturnal light.

WOOD DALE, May 13, 1971—Irene Rogozinski observed a nocturnal light.

WOODSTOCK, August 8, 1975—Nocturnal light observed.

WOODSTOCK, 1:40 a.m., May 30, 1998—Two cousins had a close encounter of the second kind, in a barnyard. (For more information see chapter 4, "The 1998 UFO Wave.")

ZIEGLER, October 5, 1973—Agnes Wehrle experienced a close encounter of the second kind.

CHAPTER 8
AREA FIVE

According to a Time/Yankelovich poll, 34 percent of Americans believe intelligent beings from other planets have visited Earth; of those, 65 percent believe a UFO crash-landed near Roswell, and 80 percent believe the U.S. government knows more about extraterrestrials than it chooses to let on.
—Time, June 23, 1997

Forget Area 51. It's Area 5: Chicago.

Oh—and the aliens from Roswell? They went to Chicago's Museum of Science and Industry.

Before you say, "Huh?" it's going to take some explaining.

By now, all America has heard of the tip-top-secret Air Force Base north of Las Vegas, near the sleepy town of Rachel, an Air Force base with no name. You've seen it, fictionalized, in the *X-Files* TV series and the movie *Men in Black*. You've also seen it on *60 Minutes*, when former employees and late employees' survivors attempted to sue the government for illegally disposing of toxic waste.

It is a real base, though the government today only reluctantly admits it, thanks to the lawsuit. It was created to test exotic new aircraft technologies. Here is where the plane most famously piloted by Gary Powers was tested and based: the U-2. Here, too, was tested its successor, the Blackbird. And most recently, the new wave of stealth aircraft were tested and based here.

Here, too, supposedly are tested even more exotic technologies, including those taken from crashed flying saucers. In support of this, there are eyewitnesses, stories from former and current employees, and photos and videos of...things beyond current known technology. A 1990 *Aviation Week* magazine reported that at Area 51 "there is substantial evidence that another family of craft exists that relies solely on exotic propulsion and aerodynamic schemes not fully understood at this time. Data pertaining to this type of vehicle are being studied by *Aviation Week* and several consultants."

But does it add up to an alien presence?

The base with no name does have unofficial names. Some call it "Dreamland," the fitting, alleged radio call sign of its airport. Others call it by the name it once had on survey maps of the area, when it was still a test range for atomic bombs, a fact that later made it ideally horrific in the eyes of those looking to site an air base off limits to the curious. The map name was "Area 51."

Forget Area 51. I think it's all at Area 5. That is, Chicago.

Yes, Area 5, the recruiting district of the Great Lakes Naval Training Center.

The navy and its Office of Naval Intelligence (ONI) have broad interests. The ONI's 1998 budget included large appropriations for, among other things, "Surface/Aerospace Surveillance and Weapons Technology" and "Space and Electronic Warfare Technology."

In fact, the official mission of the Naval Space Operations Center is to "[m]aintain a constant surveillance of space and provide space control support and space force enhancement support to the combatant commanders, their operating forces, and to other authorized Department of Defense, government and non-government organizations." It's a whole lot more than boats.

TINKER, TAILOR, SAILOR, SPY: YOUR OFFICE OF NAVAL INTELLIGENCE

The Office of Naval Intelligence has extremely broad powers and has been authorized to conduct investigations within the United States. It was founded in 1882 to collect and record "such information as may be useful...in time of war as well as in peace." During World War I, the office expanded into counterintelligence. In 1939 a secret intelligence section was created to oversee ONI spies. While the CIA has never been officially able to conduct intelligence collection within U.S. borders, the ONI was given this responsibility in 1943. In 1945 the Naval Photographic Intelligence Center was created. It would later become the government agency that evaluated UFO photos and films for the Air Force. Following World War II, while the Navy downsized, the ONI grew.

The ONI was isolated from the overall U.S. intelligence service in 1964, when the Navy developed data on the Vietnam War that was at odds with its sister intelligence agencies.

When the modern UFO era dawned, in 1947, the Air Force was officially charged with investigating UFOs, but someone else conducted parallel research. The Air Force admitted this fact in 1967 when it issued a memo from the Air Force assistant vice chief of staff, Lieutenant General Hewitt T. Wheless, which was distributed throughout the service:

"Information, not verifiable, has reached Headquarters USAF that persons claiming to represent the Air Force or *other Defense establishments* have contacted citizens who have sighted unidentified flying objects. In one reported case an individual in civilian clothes, who represented himself as a member of NORAD [North American Air Defense Command], demanded and received photos belonging to a private citizen. In another, a person in an Air Force uniform approached local police and other citizens who had sighted a UFO, assembled them in a school room and told them they did not see what they thought they saw and that they should not talk to anyone about the sighting" (emphasis added).

Wheless advised, "All military and civilian personnel and particularly Information Officers and UFO Investigating officers who hear of such reports should immediately notify their local OSI [USAF Office of Special Investigations] offices."

Fielding disguised personnel in air force uniforms was certainly beyond the capability of anyone but an intelligence agency. By definition these are spies. But from where would these chameleons come? Illinois.

In the 1970s freelance journalist Warren Smith came to Madison, Wisconsin, in response to a UFO sighting: a farmer had seen a UFO in his orchard outside the city. Smith checked into a Holiday Inn, made arrangements to visit the farmer, and found that the man had recovered a piece of metal, apparently from the UFO.

The farmer gave the metal to Smith. Smith came back to Madison. Then the farmer spoke with Smith again and said that a "fertilizer salesman" had been out, asking a lot about the UFO and the metal and not working too hard to sell fertilizer. The farmer needed to see Smith again.

No stranger to the paranoia of "ufology," Smith took the back off the TV in his hotel room and fastened the metal sample to the inside. "I asked the maids and hotel maintenance man to watch my room during my absence," Smith told Timothy Good in *Above Top Secret*. As soon as he left, though, two men with a room key went in. A maid saw them and went in a minute later, on the pretense of checking the room. She saw the two going through Smith's suitcase.

Meanwhile, Smith was talking to the farmer, who had since met with some representatives from the government who wanted the metal. The farmer had agreed, he said, based on "national security, a danger to the world, and the government's desire."

Discouraged, Smith went back to his hotel room and there encountered the two visitors. One was at the room's desk, and the other was stretched out on Smith's bed. One of the men said, "You have something we want. A farmer gave you a piece of metal the other day. Our job is to pick it up." Smith asked to see some identification.

"Name the agency and we'll produce it," the man said. "Would you like Air Force, FBI, or maybe NORAD?"

Smith was growing increasingly uncomfortable, and he had only been loaned the metal in the first place. The farmer wanted it to go to the government. Smith agreed to turn over the fragment if the men would answer a few questions. They agreed but of course didn't really offer any real information, other than that "UFOs involve more than you or any civilian can realize. They're the most important thing and perhaps the greatest hazard that mankind has ever faced." Smith turned over the metal and saw the men off. Their car had Illinois plates.

I believe they returned to the Great Lakes Naval Training Center in Chicago. There, in 1973, a gunner's mate recruited by Naval Intelligence was given triple-A security clearance and was promised a five-A clearance if he performed well for the next year and a half.

"Now, I was sequestered one night for guard duty on a Quonset hut at the northwestern end of the base," the gunner's mate told Lawrence Fawcett and Barry J. Greenwood, researchers who had made extensive use of the Freedom of Information Act to gain government documents relating to UFOs. "We were told there was highly top secret material in that Quonset hut. We were not supposed to go inside and not to look in any windows. We were to guard the place and let no one in or out without the proper identification. We were not supposed to let anyone near the place, up to a one hundred foot perimeter around it. The Quonset hut was near the lake, and it was in officer's territory. It was the older part of the base where they had used a lot of the dorms for officers who had families there. There were warehouses in and around that area.

"One night I was Officer of the Guard. I was given a letter by a messenger that I was supposed to give to the OD [Officer on Duty]. It was for his eyes only and it was a sealed envelope. I was to get a signed receipt from him. The receipt was on the front of the envelope; to do this, I had to go inside. I had to call and tell then what I was doing, and the officer was busy at that time, so it was decided that I was to be allowed inside the building to his office, have him sign the receipt, then turn around and walk out. Now this was highly unusual; normally they would come to the door and sign the receipt and I would [not] get inside, but that night the OD was busy.

"They let me in through this sliding door, a nice large metal door. I walked inside and was stopped to sign in. I was escorted down the hallway about 20 feet by three burly MPs [Military Police]. I took a turn to the right for about five feet, walked out into a warehousing area where I saw a strange craft off to my left. I was told to walk on, get my signed receipt, turn around, and leave. I was told not to pay any attention to what was going on around me.

"As I went to the doorway, where the OD was, I saw a very highly unusual craft over to my left. The craft was possibly 30 to 35 feet long, about 12 to 15 feet at its thickest part, then it tapered off in the front to a teardrop shape. I only caught it at an angular view. It looked like it did not have any seams to it. It had a bluish tint but that was only if you looked at it for a few seconds. If you looked at it and turned your eyes away real quick, all you saw were white lights, but as long as you stared at it, it took on a bluish appearance, a light bluish appearance. It was sitting on a pedestal or frame made out of four by four wooden blocks. It was held up by crossbeams underneath it and was sitting about a foot or two off the floor.

"At that time, I had turned and walked into the office where the OD was sitting. There were several people in there, nobody was talking, nobody was doing anything; everybody was watching me. They seemed nervous. I laid the envelope on the desk, did a quarter of a turn to my left, so I could not see what was in the envelope. I was scared that I might see something that I was not supposed to.

"At this time I had a very good view about halfway from the craft to the tail section. The whole craft tapered back to a very high edge. It looked as if it had a razor edge, a razor sharp edge. The bottom went about three-quarters the length of the craft and then angled sharply upward.

"I was then ordered by the Officer on Duty to take the receipt, which meant I had to turn around and face him. The envelope had disappeared, and I don't know where it went. I was told to take my receipt and leave and not say anything to anyone about what I had seen. I turned around to my left. As I did, I got a full scan of what the craft was, and then I did a very quick about-face and was escorted out.

"I finished my shift as outside duty officer, and that's all. I turned the receipt in to the officer of the deck that morning. I then slept until about four o'clock in the afternoon, and that was it."

Two months later, the gunner's mate and ONI recruit was sent to San Diego, to help outfit a submarine with missiles. "I was talking to one of the guys who was on a destroyer and it seemed as though they had tangled with some unidentified craft. He didn't know what it was. They brought it down in the Pacific in about 350 feet of water. The reason that nobody could tell if it was a craft or not is that it didn't look like anything that he had seen before. He sketched it for me. I was in a bar with him at the time, and we had a few beers, so I took the story with a grain of salt, until I saw the sketch of what the craft looked like. It was an exact copy of the same craft I had seen in Chicago. This...would have put it around June of 1973 that the craft was shot down. It was brought from San Diego by rail to Chicago, where it was worked on.... They shot it down with a surface-to-air missile, according to what the sailor said. They hit the craft but didn't destroy it. According to him, they didn't even dent it, but it sent up a concussion through the craft and whatever was inside of it was destroyed or hurt or whatever. I don't know, he didn't say. He did say that they were able to pull some sort of life form from out of it. That's all I heard from him. He did tell me that Glomar Explorer was used to extract the craft from 350 of water. And that the ship was a naval destroyer escort; destination of the vessel was Hawaii at the time of the incident."

I have a source who also heard of a recovered craft in the same specific building at Great Lakes; in fact, the source offered me confirming information not found in the story the gunner's mate told.

It has been not the Air Force but the Office of Naval Intelligence that has been conducting the real research into UFOs, and the truth has been here all along, in plain view. It has been obscured by a careful campaign of disinformation. Confirmation comes from many sources, including a former British Naval Intelligence officer, Ivan Sanderson.

THE GREAT LAKES NAVAL TRAINING CENTER

The Great Lakes Naval Training Center is the country's third-largest naval base and is the largest military installation in Illinois. In 1997, 48,000 lived on the base.

Great Lakes is a full-fledged naval base. Its command and support units include the Defense Security Service, whose official motto is "Our business is security... our promise is customer satisfaction." Its mission is to provide the Department of Defense and other federal agencies "an array of security products and services which are designed to deter and detect espionage."

After the Spanish-American War it was observed that 43 percent of the Navy's recruits came from the Midwest. To serve them, the Great Lakes Naval Training Center was founded in 1911, and since then it has trained more than three million sailors. Chicago beat out 37 other sites for the base. It originally was 172 acres and was purchased with the assistance of the Merchants Club of Chicago, which added $175,000 to the funds already appropriated by Congress. From the beginning, it was to be the largest naval training center in the world.

Today there are 1,153 buildings at Great Lakes, totaling more than 13 million square feet. The base covers 924 acres, with 59 miles of road, 44 miles of waterline, and 50 miles of sewer. There are quarters for 13,000 recruits. There is a hospital, three clinics, four dental clinics, four gyms, a golf course, and a bowling alley.

Sanderson was a writer and naturalist with an avid interest in unexplained phenomena. Sanderson was also a British Naval Intelligence operative during World War II. Eventually he was transferred to British Security Coordination and then to the British Government Services' New York office of Information and Overseas Press Analysis. He finally departed government service in 1947 and stayed in the United States to pursue his interests in natural history.

Sanderson's background in British Naval Intelligence and his subsequent New York work of course brought him into contact with U.S. Naval Intelligence, and he made and held on to relationships with ONI officers. So when he began researching his 1970 book on UFOs, *Invisible Residents,* Sanderson had some good starting points.

Sanderson visited "the heads of five departments of the Navy," and the heads of four top public-private research firms with sensitive U.S. Naval contracts whose staffs included high-ranking service personnel.

How much was finally revealed to Sanderson we may never know. Some of his contacts may have feigned ignorance to learn how much information had been leaked. Others may have told Sanderson many things that he was unable to print: Sanderson, as a former intelligence officer, always made sure to clear his information with his contacts. But his final conclusion was this:

"The poor air forces have been given the ball and, although they have carried it for two decades, said 'ball' is now a rather damp, limp, wet pulp. The navies, on the other hand, have come through in quite another manner. They were no more impelled to pronounce upon [the UFO] matter than were [other branches of the military], but, it now transpires, they really got with it."

The U.S. Navy, Sanderson wrote, "put on a fine front of obfuscation or bland indifference, and they pulled down a perfectly legitimate security curtain on all this."

The Air Force's first UFO study began officially as Project Sign, on September 23, 1947. By early September 1948, the Air Force had issued its official and top secret Estimate of the Situation: "The reported phenomena are real."

Despite this finding, Project Sign was, for scientific purposes, essentially closed. Its name—unknown to the public—was changed to Project Grudge, and its new emphasis was to downplay UFO reports. The program was later built up as project Blue Book by Air Force Captain Edward Ruppelt, but the earlier change to Grudge gave him pause.

Ruppelt was nobody's fool. During World War II he had flown submarine patrol and had received five battle stars, two theater combat ribbons, three Air Medals, and two Distinguished Flying Crosses. He held a degree in aeronautical engineering and had top-security clearance. The change from Project Sign to Project Grudge gave him some unpleasant thoughts as he took over the Air Force UFO inquiry in 1952.

"This [Grudge] period of 'mind changing' bothered me," he said. "I didn't like it because if somebody above me knew that UFOs were really spacecraft, I could make a big fool of myself if the truth came out."

That "somebody above" Ruppelt was, I believe, the Office of Naval Intelligence. Attention had already been drawn to the Navy, and to Chicago. On January 11, 1950, in a confused account, *Variety* columnist Frank Scully* reported that the dead occupants of a UFO crash in New Mexico had been sent to Chicago's Museum of Science and Industry. The story was quickly discounted. Professor Harvey B. Lemon, the museum's head of science and education, said, "Insofar as reference is made to exhibits in the museum, they are utterly without foundation in fact." Of course, it is unlikely that such specimens would have been *exhibited*.

But on April 7, 1950, *U.S. News and World Report* solved the UFO riddle! The magazine reported that the flying saucers were real and, furthermore, were our own. It stated: "An early model of these saucers was built in 1942, [and] achieved more than 100 successful test flights. That project was then taken over by the Navy in wartime. Much more advanced models now are being built."

The story, which the magazine pieced together from scientists, "private observers," and military officials—in the magazine's stilted language of the day—was this:

"A plane that could rise almost straight would not need long airfields, could be used from any cleared area just behind front-line troops or from the deck of any Navy combat ship. If that plane, in addition, had great speed and more maneuverability, it could probably outfly any conventional aircraft."

The description of the craft? "Exactly 105 feet in diameter, circular in shape. They have what appear to be jet nozzles arranged all around the outer rim, just below the center of gravity. They are made of a

---

* Yes, Scully, one of the first journalists to look at the UFO phenomena, became the namesake for the character of Dana Scully on television's *X-Files*. While many of his findings were immediately discounted and may possibly have been the result of disinformation campaigns, today some of his data is being confirmed.

metal alloy, with a dull whitish color. There are no rudders, ailerons, or other protruding surfaces, From the side the saucers appear about 10 feet thick.... They are built in three layers, with the center layer slightly larger in diameter than the other two."

More outrageous claims! So what was the source? "Qualified observers of saucers in flight—commercial airline pilots, fighter pilots who have chased these aircraft, trained airplane spotters, high ranking Army and Air Force spotters." But more than that, "[i]t is backed by exact measurement made by a group of scientists last April near White Sands Proving Ground base, with instruments set up to observe high altitude balloons, who suddenly observed a saucer and tracked it for several minutes, thereby getting reliable data on its size, speed, altitude and maneuverability."

If we believe the story for a minute, who would have leaked such vital information? Who would have jeopardized the Navy's top secret project so soon after World War II?

Here's the smoking gun: it was the Navy itself. The scientists near White Sands were from the Office of Naval Research. On April 24, 1949, near Arrey, New Mexico, an Office of Naval Research (ONR) aeronautical engineer, J. Gordon Vaeth, and five technicians were tracking a weather balloon when they observed a whitish elliptical object. It was much higher than the balloon. Viewed through a theodolite, a 25-power telescope with instruments that give an object's azimuth and elevation (horizontal and vertical positions), it appeared to be two and a half times as long as it was wide and was estimated to be about 56 miles above the earth, 100 feet long, and traveling at 420 miles per hour. After being tracked for 60 seconds, the object quickly ascended out of sight. *The report was not made public until 1956.*

I believe that the Navy put out the story of its creation of flying saucers to mask its study of flying saucers. And while it seems unlikely at this distant date, it was the branch of service best qualified to undergo such research, not the Air Force. *U.S. News and World Report* recorded why:

"Big spending on missile aircraft centers in the Navy now, too. More than twice as many dollars were spent by the Navy last year as by the Air Force on secret guided-missile research. There is no public accounting for these millions, the government funds aside from atomic energy dollars that still are spent with great secrecy."

In short, the magazine concluded, the indications pointed to the "research centers of the U.S. Navy's vast guided-missile project as the scene of present flying-saucer development. That project has the scientists, the engineers, the dollars, the motive, and the background of early Navy development of saucer-type aircraft. This likelihood will remain, despite any future denials by the navy front office, until secrecy is lifted on the big missile program."

The Navy did indeed deny the claims, pointing to the very real XF5U "Flying Flapjack," an unsuccessful experimental aircraft, as the possible source for such stories (the Air Force would much later develop a ducted-air disk-shaped hover car, which it similarly blamed for UFO reports, though it never got more than a few feet off the ground). At the time, the XF5U sounded like a good candidate for mistaken identity, but since then it has been declassified. It was not the Navy's ungainly XF5U, a half-oval with four huge, counterrotating propellers, to which the magazine had been referring but another mystery craft.

So here was what had happened: the Navy leaked the story that it had created the UFOs itself. It then denied the story and turned up a real, possible reason for the stories, the XF5U. Having done so, any actual future leaks about Navy UFO research could be laughed off.

As for the Air Force's flying saucer research, it would once again be cut, dramatically. In January 1953, a panel of scientists convened at the CIA to evaluate Blue Book's UFO evidence, including an exhaustive study of UFO flight patterns conducted by Air Force Major Dewey Fournet, which concluded that UFOs were extraterrestrial. The Naval Photographic Intelligence Center presented a UFO film taken near Trementon, Utah, by a Navy Chief Photographer. The lab's conclusion was that the film showed intelligently controlled vehicles that were not airplanes or birds.

The panel decided that all the evidence was not enough to conclude that we are not alone. It did, however, recommend that the Blue Book's size be quadrupled, with a budget to match. And while it recommended that civilian UFO groups be surveilled—for fear that the belief in UFOs could create a menace manipulated by the Soviet Union*—the panel said that the public should be told all the details of every phase of the investigation. The recommendation was reported to the National Security Council, made up of the heads of all U.S. intelligence agencies.

---

* This was the Robertson Panel, named for its chair, H. P. Robertson, head of the Defense Department's Weapons Systems Evaluation Group. Its top secret report stated that "such groups...should be watched because of their potentially great influence on mass thinking if widespread sightings should occur. The apparent irresponsibility and the apparent use of such groups for subversive purposes should be kept in mind."

HEAR NO EVIL, SEE NO UFO

Besides the Navy, every branch of the military, the FBI, and every intelligence agency have a wealth of UFO documents that have been recovered by researchers through the Freedom of Information Act; the National Security Agency itself admits to holding 135 UFO documents, though it will release none (since doing so "could seriously jeopardize the work of the agency and the security of the United States"). But the U.S. Navy has very little—or so it says. Reason enough to be suspicious! And the Navy's blindness to UFOs apparently extends to UFO encounters that imperil the public.

At 11:37 p.m. on June 23, 1950, Northwest Airlines flight 2501 was 37 minutes from Milwaukee, 3,500 feet over Battle Creek, Michigan. At that moment Captain Robert C. Lind broadcast a typical position report. Everything was fine. On board were 55 passengers, including a General Mills vice president, an AT&T vice president and his family, and a priest.

Roughly an hour and a half later, at Whitefish Bay, near Milwaukee, two police officers looked out over Lake Michigan and saw a red light. They watched it for about 10 minutes. They had never seen anything like it, and they reported it to the Coast Guard.

The Coast Guard Milwaukee Station sent a ship out into the lake. They did not see any strange lights, but they did find a U.S. Navy vessel. The Coast Guard captain asked the Navy captain if he'd seen anything. "No." What were they doing out so late? "Maneuvers."

According to the June 25, 1950, Chicago Tribune, the naval vessel had not seen Northwest flight 2501. As a matter of fact, no one has ever seen Northwest flight 2501 since. It disappeared, 37 minutes from Milwaukee. The Coast Guard didn't know that until the next morning. They launched a search at dawn. Eventually even the Navy was called in, and they used secret radar and sonar devices to find the underwater wreckage. It was never found. No bodies were ever found. No clothing, floatation devices, luggage, not so much as an oil slick.

Unlikely? Or a lie? The flight would have passed directly over the Navy ship. After a year, the Civilian Aeronautics Board delivered its findings: "The Board determines that there is not sufficient evidence upon which to make a determination of probable cause.... None of the radio communications received from the flight, including the last, contained any mention of trouble." The possibility "that this accident resulted from some mechanical failure seems to be remote."

As a result...well, you'll never guess. Blue Book was cut, dramatically. It became the work of one lieutenant and an airman first class.

Blue Book limped along, primarily as a public relations exercise, until December 1969, when the Air Force closed it. But work continued in other government agencies; Northwestern University astronomer J. Allen Hynek, Blue Book's longtime civilian adviser, himself cleared for top secret materials, wrote of the Blue Book's last years in the 1960s, "One time when I inquired into the specifics of a certain case, I was told by the Pentagon's chief scientist that he had been advised by those at a much higher level to tell me 'not to pursue the matter further.' One can make of that what one will."

As for the stories about Nevada's Area 51? It's another intentional distraction from the actual UFO-research workplaces. Almost all we know of the alleged alien spacecraft at Area 51 comes from one man, Bob Lazar, whose credentials are fuzzy except for one verifiable fact: according to the Social Security Administration, he's a former employee of the Office of Naval Intelligence.

Area 51 is just disinformation. The stories were created to draw attention away from a neighboring base, a former Navy Auxiliary airfield, constructed, according to several sources in conversations with researcher and former Air Force colonel Wendelle Stevens, by a Navy construction battalion. The base is south of Dreamland and was created in 1951, with most of the new facility being installed underground. And it is from there that the exotic aircraft reported and photographed by so many originate.

Or used to. The latest rumor is that because of all the attention paid to Area 51, research into exotic flight technologies has been moved to a former biological-warfare testing site in Colorado.

And, of course, there remains Chicago.

CHAPTER 9
BIGFOOT

Jennifer Rigsby was 15. She lived near Reevesville, about 10 miles north of Metropolis. In early 1990 she was staying at the rural home of a friend named Sheila.

"At about 1 or 2 a.m. we both had to pee and decided to just go to the back door so we wouldn't wake her parents," Jennifer recalled. "The backyard was a field of head-high weeds that had grown up about five feet from the door. When we had almost finished 'doing our duty,' we heard strange noises like nothing we ever heard before. It sounded like growling, snorting, and huffing and was about 30 feet away.

"It seemed like forever that we stood there listening to it. Either we were trying to figure out what was out there or couldn't believe what we were hearing. My pants were still around my knees.

"Then it started to run toward us. It definitely had two feet. It came crashing through the weeds and sounded like a person running, but with heavier footfalls. We ran for the door not looking back. I personally didn't want to see it. It still was chasing us as we slammed the back door, too close for comfort.

"When we slammed the door, I could smell something terrible in the air. We ran into [Sheila's] room and a couple of minutes later we heard it outside her window. We woke her parents, but they didn't believe us and we could not find any prints around the backyard or her window, I guess because the ground was dry.

"I know what I heard, and my friend believes what she saw and heard. No one will ever change our minds."

Bigfoot has been seen many times in the Great Lakes region. In Michigan City, Indiana, in the summer of 1839, a "wild child" reportedly haunted that city's Fish Lake, "setting up the most frightful and hideous yells," according to an early press account. Today we would call it a child Bigfoot. In Illinois, the large, furry creature on two legs goes by several regional names, including "Big Mo," "Big Muddy Monster," and "Cohomo."

Around 1912, near Effingham—more than a decade after the fact—Beaulah Schroat recalled that from time to time in the first decade of the twentieth century, her brothers saw hairy creatures near their home. On July 25, 1929, near Elizabeth, a "huge gorilla" was seen in the woods near town.

While hunting squirrels near Mount Vernon in the summer of 1941, the Reverend Lepton Harpole saw "a large animal that looked something like a baboon," which leaped from a tree. The creature walked toward the cleric, who struck it with the barrel of his gun. Harpole finally scared the animal away by firing a few shots into the air. More sightings would occur a year later, in early spring.

After leaving tracks and screaming in the night, the ill-tempered beast sighted a year before apparently killed a dog. A search was organized for the creature, reportedly driving it toward Okaw and Muddy River, where a driver saw it cross a road. It was said that the animal could jump 20 to 40 feet! (We'll have more to say about this phenomenal leaping Bigfoot in another chapter.)

In November 1962, east of Decatur, Steven Collins, Robert Earle, and two other men saw a gray Bigfoot standing in a creek off East William Strett Road. In May a year later, in Centreville, police received 50 calls about a "half-man, half-horse."

Around 1965, in Trenton, Brian Schwaz and Kevin Nowak found 14-inch Bigfoot tracks leading across a field and into some farmland woods. The tracks were two inches deep, while the young men's own prints sank in only a quarter-inch.

On September 22, 1965, in Decatur, two men and two women parked in a lover's lane area near the city saw a Bigfoot approach their car. It was black and "manlike." It wasn't a stunt designed to heighten romance, since the frightened men immediately took the women into town. They then returned to search for whatever it was. They saw it again and fled to make a police report. Officers said that the young men were sincerely "well frightened."

August 11, 1968, near Chittyville: in late July and early August, area residents had noticed that their dogs were sometimes upset during the night, barking loudly and "carrying on." Soon the apparent reason was revealed. Tim Bullock, 22, of West Frankfort, and Barbara Smith, 17, of Carterville, were driving north of town when they saw a 10-foot black creature with a round, hairy face. It threw dirt through their car window, and the two left to find the police. On investigation, officers found a depression in the grass, apparently a nest. (Such nests seem to be typical of the Great Lakes Bigfoot.)

Near Salt Creek, on July 9, 1970, Don Ennis, Beecher Lamb, Larry Faircloth, and Bob Hardwick, all age 18, were camping in a 10-acre field near Farmer City when they saw a Bigfoot circling their campfire, its eyes reflecting the light. The creature ran away on two legs.

In early August 1970, near Waynesville, teenagers Steve Rich, George Taylor, and Monti Shafer saw a furry, upright creature on the Daryl Finger farm, two miles northeast of the community. A few days later, at 9:30 p.m. on August 16, north of Waynesville, construction workers Dan Lindsey and Mike Anderson saw an upright creature near the Kickapoo Creek bridge on Route 136. It was six feet tall, brown, had stooped shoulders, and was "trotting" along the bank of the creek.

While driving, Vicki Otto saw an "ape running in the ditch" in early August 1970, near Bloomington.

In the early 1970s, sometime between 1970 and 1972, a very unusual set of circumstances occurred near Pekin. An anonymous witness tells the story:

"I lived in the country at the time, about two miles from the Mackinaw River, which is a pretty heavily wooded area. I was sitting on the ground, shooting at birds, and it was getting dark out. I was about 150 to 200 feet from the barn, when all of a sudden the barn door opened and something started coming out.

"I do not recall any details about what I saw because I was so scared! I do know that whatever it was, it took up the whole space of the barn door. It was dark, so if it was a black man, he would have to have been a large black man—and I am not convinced that this is what I saw.

"The reason I say this is that although Pekin is a pretty good-sized town, around 30,000 people then, and not too much larger now, [it] is a town that does not have very many blacks that live in it. At that time Pekin did not have a black population at all, so it would seem almost unlikely to me that [that] is what I saw.

"I ran into the house right way. I was around 10 or 12 at the time, and we locked the doors. The dogs started barking real soon after I saw whatever it was, and barked for about three solid hours, more than I had ever heard them bark before or have ever heard dogs bark.

"Nobody else saw it, but a friend saw a shadow go across the barn when he looked out the window. We called the sheriff's office, and a couple of officers went out and looked but did not find anything.

"I cannot recall how much time later, but within a couple or so months, me and my brother and cousin found the front half of a pig, down about 150 to 200 feet behind the barn. There was [sic] no bones of the pig left, just half of a young pig, probably about six months old.

"Something unusual about this is that there were no animals around us that could have done this, and if a human was going to do this, I am sure he would have stolen the whole pig, not just half of it. At least, I would."

Late May 1972, near Peoria: Randy Emert, age 18, said that he and his friends twice saw a large hairy creature near Cole Hollow Road. It stood between eight and 12 feet tall, was whitish, and moved quickly. Several times the young people heard the animal let out "a screech kind of like an old steam engine whistle, only more human." The young people suspected that it lived in a hole dug beneath a nearby abandoned house. They didn't report their sightings, Emert said, because "people would think we're crazy." Whatever the creature was or is, it left very unusual tracks—each foot had only three toes. While this is very unlike Bigfoot, reports of large upright creatures from Wisconsin, Illinois, and Minnesota often do leave tracks with only three toes (see Chapter 10, "The Windy City's Killer Kangaroo"). Emert stressed to the *Pekin Daily Times* that he was not "doing this for publicity." As others saw the same or a similar creature in the same vicinity, it soon became known as "Cohomo," for "Cole Hollow Road Monster."

On May 25, the East Peoria Police Department logged 200 calls reporting the creature, including one from Leroy Summer, who saw a 10-foot white Bigfoot standing near the Illinois River levee. Also that night, in East Peoria, two men saw a smelly, 10-foot Bigfoot. In another sighting, the creature destroyed a fence.

The forward-thinking officers vowed that they would administer a lie-detector test to anyone reporting the monster. Cairo Police Commissioner James Dailey similarly promised that observers in his own jurisdiction would have to submit to breath tests to determine their alcohol intake. The *Pekin Daily Times,* in a remarkable display of what it perceived to be astute thinking, pointed out that the creature, also reported in Louisiana, would have had to travel 165 airline miles, grow three feet, and change colors for it to have been seen as described in all the places reported. It apparently never occurred to reporters that there may have been more than one creature.

By July 26, so many sightings had been made that about 100 volunteers organized to search for Cohomo. Many were "armed to the hilt," according to the *Pekin Daily Times.* Tazewell County sheriff's officers dispersed the searchers after Carl R. Harris accidentally shot himself in the leg with a .22-caliber pistol. The bullet passed through Harris's right thigh and lodged in his calf. Harris said he'd brought the gun to protect himself. He was hospitalized overnight, as deputies continued to patrol the area.

Sheriff Donahue said that he had heard from a farmer that a large deer had been seen in the area and guessed that it had been responsible for the unusual tracks. But deer or monster, "We do not need any help from any citizens," Donahue noted, "especially those with any guns or other weapons."

At 7:35 p.m. the next day, an anonymous woman caller told sheriff's officers that she had seen the monster while she was picking berries near an old coal mine on Route 98. She was so scared as she ran away that she forgot her purse. Deputies went to the scene but found nothing.

Perhaps coincidentally, a Eureka man reported to the sheriff's department that about an hour later, at 8:30, he and his family were celebrating a birthday in Fondulac Park, in East Peoria, when they saw some strange lights descend vertically, landing behind some trees. The lights left a vapor trail.

The same night East Peoria Police said that "two reliable citizens" had reported seeing Cohomo swimming in the Illinois River. They were close enough to observe that it was 10 feet tall, smelled awful, had long, gray U-shaped ears, a red mouth, sharp teeth, and thumbs with long second joints. They said it "looked like a cross between an ape and a caveman." (The same day, in Cairo, a 10-foot white Bigfoot was reported standing on the banks of the Ohio River.)

At about this time, a farming family near Salem had its own encounter. An anonymous witness recalled that one morning his mother had seen "a large beige creature at the edge of a woods area, about 100 yards from our house. The house was surrounded on three sides by cornfields, and a densely wooded area surrounded that." The nearest family was two miles away.

The corn had already been harvested, so the view from the house was clear. The woman was speaking on the phone to her mother when the family's dogs, both inside and out, began howling. On the phone the whole time, the woman walked to the edge of the screen porch and saw a large animal, crouching. Suddenly it straightened, looking into the house.

The woman's mother said over the phone not to go outside. The woman called to the dogs, some 500 feet away. After 15 to 20 seconds, the creature just walked into the woods.

Earlier that summer, the family had found a trampled "nest" on the edge of one of the cornfields. Perhaps significantly, they moved after only a year on the farm.

On May 6, 1973, at Enfield: after nearby sightings of a three-legged creature, Rick Rainbow and three others said they saw a more conventional apelike creature near an abandoned house. It was grayish and five and a half feet tall.

Three sightings were made in Madison County between June 4 and June 8, 1973, in woods east of Edwardsville. Each time a red-eyed, smelly, upright creature was seen. It was described as 5 feet 8 inches tall and broad-shouldered. In one case, a witness told police that the creature had ripped his shirt and scratched his chest.

June 25, 1973, near Murphysboro: Randy Needham and Judy Johnson were parked near the Big Muddy River when they saw a seven-foot white Bigfoot with muddy hair. It shrieked, the two drove away, and large tracks were later found. The next day, Christian Baril, age four, Randy Creath, and Ceryl Ray had a similar sighting. Christian was the first, claiming to have seen "a big white ghost" in a yard. Ten minutes later Creath and Ray saw a seven-foot white Bigfoot, with muddy hair and pink eyes. It stood and watched the humans, and then walked off through some trees. The creature left a strong "sewer" odor and was later tracked by police using a trained dog.

Around June 1973, Edwardsville: three reports were made of a smelly, red-eyed Bigfoot in the woods. It chased observers and even clawed one man's chest.

July 4, 1973, Murphysboro: here's another of my favorite sightings. The miniature confounded the gigantic when carnival workers saw a Bigfoot staring at Shetland ponies.

January 1974, Aurora: the creature locally called "Big Mo" was sighted. It was large, dirty white, and left large footprints.

July 1974, Murphysboro: the area's creature was seen once again.

Autumn 1974, Carol Stream: several people saw a Bigfoot with glowing red eyes and a gray-tipped head, apparently at night. It left footprints.

Jennifer Rigsby's encounter, outlined at the beginning of this chapter, was actually her second. The first was in October 1989.

"Both [sightings] occurred in the wooded hills near the home where I grew up. The first incident was at an abandoned cabin where four friends and I hiked one night. Three of my friends were on the porch when they ran inside screaming, 'We gotta get the hell outta here, we just saw something.' They were frantic, and when I finally got them to tell me what they saw, I didn't believe them at first—until I saw the two 'macho' guys about to cry. They said it was about 7 feet tall, [had] dark hair, and sort of hunched over. They heard it in the woods to the left and saw it run across the trail into the woods to the right. Needless to say, we got the hell out of there and never went back to the cabin at night.

"In the first incident, it was either oblivious to our presence or was running away. In the second incidence it was chasing us, its intent not known, but it probably wasn't going to have a pleasant conversation with us. A few years after these experiences my friend and I found out that one of her neighbors had a close encounter with 'it.' She and her friend were camping near the edge of the same woods in a camper. They heard the same sounds outside their camper. They thought maybe it was her brother playing a trick so they said, "Go away." Then the camper started to sway and the thing started to pound at the sides and the door. They yelled for their mom, and when she came out of the house it ran into the woods. There was [sic] dents and scratches left on the camper."

In May or June 1979, a young man had a similar encounter with the creature, near the town of Westchester, in Cook County.

"When I was a junior in high school, a friend and I decided to skip school one day. The school I attended was quite a way from my home, and we decided to spend our day walking to my house and stopping in stores to look around and get something to eat along the way.

"As we started to get close to my home I realized it was too early in the day to go home, so I suggested that we go to the nearby woods and hang out till it got a little later in the day. The area of the woods that we went to has a large hill with railroad tracks to the left, a wooded area to the right, [and] a path going along the right side of the bottom of the hill. On the other side of the hill is a creek.

"We had walked along the path going maybe 50 yards or so from the road when my friend stopped suddenly and said in a low voice, 'What is that?' I immediately looked up the path and saw a very large hairy animal running away from us down the path. It had black hair that—from what I could see—covered its whole body.

"The scariest thing was that it ran just like a man would run on two legs, with arms swinging, only much faster than any man could run. The sight of it scared us so badly that we both dived to the ground while continuing to watch it run away. The whole episode actually lasted about 10 seconds or so. As soon as the creature was out of sight we got up and nervously headed out of the woods. I had to keep looking back because even though it had run a good distance from us, I knew that it could easily catch us if it wanted to. Both my friend and I decided not to talk about what we had seen with anyone else, and as I recall we never discussed it again."

In the same county at about the same time, a very odd sighting was made by a group of young people:

"This was the second time that I had seen the creature which I believe to be a Bigfoot. I previously [had seen] something out of the corner of my eye while walking in the bushes.

"One summer night in 1979 I was hanging out with two of my friends. We were all about 17 years old, and we were looking for something to do. We decided to go to a store a mile or so away. On the way back we were confronted by some older guys in their 20s. They were drunk and were trying to scare us, which they did. We all split up and ran for it.

"After hiding out for a while I headed back to my friend's house hoping to meet up with them. One of my friends was getting back about the same time as I was. After we caught our breath we started to look around for our other friend. Of course we thought the worst. We heard a sound coming from the bushes that were directly in front of his house. We called his name but didn't get an answer. I thought he was hiding on us, so I walked over to the bushes to take a look. The problem was that there weren't any streetlights on our block, and on a dark night like that I couldn't see very well.

"I started to walk through the bushes, checking behind them, but I didn't see anything. I started to walk out of the bushes when something caught my eye. I almost stopped, but I just had a bad feeling about it and decided to ignore it. I told my friend I didn't see anything. We started to walk to my house, which was across the street. As we were crossing the street I heard what sounded like a chain dragging on the ground. Because it was so dark and I couldn't see what was making the sound, again I thought it might be my friend.

"Suddenly I saw something very large coming directly toward me, taking very long strides. I couldn't see any details of its face, just the outline of its body. It was very big, at least eight feet tall, and it was hairy. I couldn't tell what color it was. It was growling as it came toward us. By the sound of its growl, I could tell that it was very angry.... I believe there may have been a smaller Bigfoot in [the bushes], possibly a child Bigfoot. Perhaps when the Bigfoot saw me walking through the bushes it came over to protect the smaller one.

"My friend and I screamed, turned around, and ran as fast as we possibly could. We ran up his driveway and into the side door. I kept running into the house, but he stopped to lock the door and look out the window. He screamed out that he saw it run down his neighbor's driveway and go in back of their garage.

"We told [my friend's] dad what was going on, and he was very skeptical, but he could see that we were very frightened. We kept looking out the front window hoping our other friend would get back. After a while we saw him coming down the street toward the house. We yelled for him to run in the house, but as I recall he wouldn't do it. By the way we were acting he must have thought we were going to play a trick on him. We ended up running out to get him and convinced him to come into the house right away. Of course, he wanted to talk about what had happened with the drunken guys chasing us—while we were wanting to talk about this creature.

"Needless to say he wouldn't believe us. After hearing us talk about the incident with the creature, his younger brother told his dad that he had been chased by something similar while he was in the woods a week or so before. I also told him about a creature I had seen two weeks before, running in the distance, at those same woods. Now his dad, who was a avid gun collector and former special-forces member, started to take us seriously. He got a rifle and told us to show him where we had seen the creature.

"We took him to the woods, where he parked his truck, taking his rifle and flashlight, and headed into the woods. He gave us a lot of grief about it, but neither me nor my friends would go with him. My friend's younger brother did go. We sat in his truck for a half an hour or so, praying that this thing wouldn't attack us, or his dad and brother. Finally they came back after being unable to find anything. At last that night came to an end."

* * *

Assuming it's real, where does Bigfoot come from?

We have always seen large, upright, furry creatures—even if we didn't want to. The Delaware Indians called creatures like Bigfoot "Alligewi," after the Allegheny River. According to Delaware legend, the Alligewi once tried to migrate to the east, into the traditional Delaware territories. The Delaware went to war with the Alligewi and fought them down the Ohio River, then up the Mississippi, and then to Minnesota. The story is then picked up by the Minnesota Sioux, who have a legend about a race of giants that appeared there—and were killed. Similarly, George E. Powell, writing in 1907, said that 27 years earlier he had heard oral histories representing such a battle to have occurred 200 years earlier. The dead were strangers; they were slain by Ojibwa; the story had come from a 100-year-old Ojibwa.

In Minnesota the giants were called Windigo. The Reverend Peter Jones was a missionary traveling through what later became Minnesota in 1831, and he knew firsthand of the Windigo. An Ojibwa himself, he was taken from his tribe and was taught by missionaries. But he never forgot his early childhood, when he had "often listened with wonder and deep attention to the stories related of the waindegoos [sic], or giants. They are represented as beings tall as pine trees.... In their travels they pull down and turn aside immense forests, as a man would the high grass as he passes through.

"They are said to live on human flesh, and whenever they meet an Indian are sure to have a good meal; being also invulnerable to the shot of an arrow or bullet, they are the constant dread of the Indians. Persons who have been known to eat human flesh from starvation are also called waindegoos, after the giants."

Indeed, "the Windigo are powerful giants," wrote Charles Brown, of the State Historical Society of Wisconsin, who collected Ojibwa Windigo stories in 1927. It was part animal, a wild "man" who left footprints twice the normal size. The legends reported that the Windigo killed Indians for food, cut them up, and boiled them in their kettles. "The belief in them still persists," Brown wrote.

Possibly, the Windigo legends refer to an earlier form of man— caveman. Neanderthal lived about 75,000 years ago and then inexplicably vanished. Could Native Americans have recalled the Neanderthal? The Ojibwa and Dakota tribal memories extended far enough back to embrace the woolly mammoth, after all. Elephantlike figures pepper the tribes' art, incredible as that may seem. And earlier forms of man have been known to have lived alongside manlike cousins. In France, archaeologists have for decades been puzzled by the fact that the Neanderthal and modern man lived side by side. Could the Indian legends tell of a race of distant relatives to man who once, at least, really did exist?

It would help, of course, if we had some hard evidence. This is the constant cry of skeptics, and rightfully so. It is one of my beliefs that we have abundant evidence of unexplained phenomena but that the data are difficult to retrieve, organize, and analyze. Early excavations, long ignored, offer proof. On August 12, 1896, the *St. Paul Globe* reported that "a huge man" was dug up at Lake Koronis, Minnesota. Indeed, that state seems to have had more than its share of disinterred giants: in Warren, in 1882, ten "gigantic bodies"; at Chatfield, seven 8-foot skeletons, with skulls showing receding foreheads. In La Crescent, 52 mounds were excavated. "When opened they have been found to contain human remains of men of large stature," reads the geological report. At Dresbach, around 1885, Indian mounds yielded 8-foot skeletons. Some 600 sets of "large human bones" were also excavated in Fillmore County. At Moose Island Lakes, an 1861 survey noted the recovery of 7-foot skeletons from mounds. At Pine City, a "gigantic" skeleton was exhumed. At Rainy River, in 1896, a 9-foot skeleton was found.

These finds are extremely problematic. Science does not attempt to fit them into the geological record but instead views each as a unique, freakish circumstance that can be ignored. After all, from where would such creatures come?

At least 40 million years ago there were indeed primates in America, but only in Central and South America, where they evolved in a manner very similar to that of their Old-World relatives; they are small monkeys and are unlikely to have given rise to a native population of Windigo, or—as it is called by Pacific Coast Indians—Sasquatch.

So if not from native stock, from where did the Windigo arise? Anthropologist Myra Shackley has pointed out, quite rightly, that since "there were no North American primates to evolve into Sasquatch, it would have evolved somewhere else and migrated to North America."

Of course, the European fossil record does present numerous candidates for what possibly evolved into the Windigo. The Neanderthal is easily ruled out; even given evolution, Neanderthal is far too small. (Several scholars have very effectively argued Neanderthal's survival in Asia, however, accounting for stories of the Abominable Snowman and similar creatures there.)

There is, however, an older form of man, *Gigantopithecus*, which evolved in Asia at least 9 million years ago and survived until at least one million years ago. It is possible that *Gigantopithecus* could have crossed a land bridge between Siberia and North America, a trip of merely 52 miles.

Shackley suggests that such a *Gigantopithecus* migration occurred before the beginning of the Ice Age, 1.8 million years ago. By comparison, *Homo sapiens,* modern man, those we know today as the Native Americans and Eskimo, probably migrated during two relatively recent periods: 36,000 to 32,000 years ago, and again 28,000 to 13,000 years ago.

If so, they've been here longer than even the Native Americans. And maybe the shoe was on the other Bigfoot at the time: perhaps the peaceful, furry giants were astounded by the occassional sighting of small, smooth-skinned men and women passing into their territories.

CHAPTER 10
THE WINDY CITY'S KILLER KANGAROO

"My partner got kicked pretty bad in the legs," Chicago Police Officer Michael Byrne told reporters. "He smacks pretty good, but we got in a few good punches to the head, and he must have felt it."

Officers Leonard Ciagi and Byrne had answered the early-morning call, and at about 3:30 a.m. on October 18, 1974, they had cornered their growling suspect at the end of a dark alley on Chicago's northwest side. The perpetrator was only five feet tall, but it soon "started to scream and get vicious" as the police fumbled with their handcuffs.

More squad cars arrived, but it was too late. The suspect leaped over a fence and jumped down the street. The kangaroo remained at large.

This is a scene right out of a Warner Bros. cartoon, one where Sylvester the cat tries to beat up a huge "mouse," which turns out to be a pugnacious kangaroo. It is ridiculous, but I think the theme of mistaken identity is being mimicked in real life: this is no kangaroo.

The 1974 encounter by Chicago Police was actually the kangaroo-like creature's second brush with the law. The first was in July 1971, when a kangaroo was sighted on the grounds of Northwestern University by campus police.

These were not isolated incidents. Illinois, along with Wisconsin and Minnesota, seems to have a pack of aggressive creatures that at least resemble kangaroos. The stories go back at least a hundred years. The same day as Byrne and Ciagi's fight with the kangaroo, another—or the same one—was seen around Belmont and Oak Park. The next day, at 7 a.m., newspaper carrier Kenneth Grieshamer, age 13, was standing on the corner of Sunnyside and Mulligan Streets when he heard a car squealing its brakes. He turned and saw a kangaroo just a few feet away.

"He looked at me, I looked at him, and then he hopped off," Grieshamer said.

An hour later, two boys near Austin and Eastwood Roads saw a kangaroo. And at 6 p.m. police received a call from a person who claimed to have seen one at Belmont and Mango Avenues. The next morning brought further reports from citizens who reported that a kangaroo was rummaging through their garbage cans! On October 23, a kangaroo was again seen, this time in Chicago's Schiller Woods, near Irving Park Road.

On the evening of November 1, Plano Police Officer John Orr was driving on Riverview Road, just outside city limits, when he saw a kangaroo leap eight feet from an adjacent cornfield. It landed in the middle of the road, where it was caught in the lights of Orr's car. "If I hadn't slowed down, I would have hit him," Orr said. "My cousin was in the car behind me, and when she saw him, she just plain ran off the road."

The next night, at about 9 p.m., 17-year-olds Jerry Wagner, Steve Morton, and Shawne Clark spotted a kangaroo in the middle of Shafer Road, again in Plano. "We almost ran over it," Wagner said. "It jumped onto the road about 20 feet ahead of us. I was on the passenger side in the front seat and I pointed it out to Shawne and Steve, and all three of us saw it. It landed on the road near the intersection with the main road, and there was no traffic. It sat up on its haunches, as kangaroos do, and then jumped over a fence about five feet high and disappeared into the woods."

A half-hour later, the kangaroo or one like it had apparently made its way 50 miles east, back to Chicago. In the 5600 block of South New

England Avenue, Cathy Battaglia and Len Zeglicz, ages 17 and 19, saw what they at first thought was a large dog. Then it hopped down the street.

The next morning, November 3, Frank Kocherver, 21, saw a kangaroo near a forest preserve on Chicago's northwest side. It leaped into the woods.

On November 4, a truck driver saw a deer and something that was *not* a deer as he pulled over next to a field near Plano. Of the strange animal, he said, "Its prints in the mud of the field are different, and I think it is a kangaroo."

On November 6, a truck driver near Lansing had to swerve off the road to avoid hitting a kangaroo. A wave of Indiana sightings followed six days later.

Half a year later, at 7 a.m. on July 14, 1975, Rosemary Hopwood was driving on Route 128, south of Dalton City, where she also saw something that she thought at first was a dog. As she neared, she saw it was a kangaroo, walking on all fours. Then it moved across the road and sat up. It was about two and a half feet tall standing, about five and a half feet long when on all four legs, and was beige. Its ears were pointed and its tail was long and thick. It disappeared into a cornfield. The same month, Dequoin farmer Kevin Luthi and others also saw a five-foot kangaroo in a cornfield, but Luthi did not immediately report it for fear of ridicule.

On April 26, the kangaroo was in Rock Island, where it was seen by Harry Masterson, 25, who was walking his dog.

"I looked across the street and there it was, a kangaroo," he said. "It came hopping through the yard. The kangaroo and I stood there looking at each other for about a minute. Then it turned around and went hopping away, off to the north." He ran inside to get his wife and mother-in-law, who came out just in time to see the creature leaping away.

So we are left with an aggressive kangaroo that seems fascinated with roadways and who forages for garbage—all distinctly unkangaroo traits, one would think. But if the witnesses are mistaken, then what was it they saw? What other mysterious creature is upright? Bigfoot?

This behavior is just as out of character for Bigfoot. I think that the problem is just the reverse. I believe that in some cases what has been turned in as a Bigfoot report is, in fact, that of a mystery kangaroo. This would help to explain some reports of Bigfoot in Illinois that are problematic, such as the 1942 sightings near Mt. Vernon in which the creature was said to be able to leap as much as 40 feet. Some of the earliest U.S. reports of Bigfoot by European settlers present similar descriptions. From the 1880s to 1900, sightings near Myrtle Point, Oregon, described a creature "as having the appearance of a man—a very good-looking man—is nine feet in height with a low forehead, hair hanging down near his eyes, and his body covered with a prolific growth of hair, which nature has provided for his protection." Its footprints measured 18 inches. With its "catlike agility, which has always been a leading characteristic," the creature moved around by leaping, giving it the nickname "Kangaroo Man."

In fact, kangaroos, or something like them, have appeared in many parts of the central United States. Two kangaroos were sighted near the Anoka County Fairgrounds near Coon Rapids, Minnesota, from 1957 to 1967. In January 1934, an incredibly fast-killing kangaroo attacked dogs, geese, and ducks in rural Tennessee. The *Chattanooga Daily Times* concluded, "There is absolutely no doubt about these facts. A kangaroo-like beast visited the community and killed dogs...and that's all there is to it."

This aggressive behavior is also a trait belonging to what has been labeled a werewolf in southeastern Wisconsin. In 1972, in Fort Atkinson, Wisconsin, such a creature was observed attacking a horse. "It took a swat at the horse and left a gash across the chest—30 inches from one shoulder to the other," said David Gjetson, of the Wisconsin Department of Natural Resources' Wildlife Department.

In 1992 a similar creature attacked a car driven by two women near Elkhorn, Wisconsin. It leapt onto the trunk and left "deep claw marks" on the metal. There are many similar stories.

Besides werewolf sightings, Wisconsin has its share of kangaroo reports, which date back to 1899, and they rival Bigfoot reports in number. In 1978 tracks found in association with a sighting in Waukesha County, next to Milwaukee, were around 6 inches long and 3 inches wide. Photos of plaster casts made from the tracks lead me to believe that whatever left them could possibly account for the bizarre "three-toed," webbed tracks reported as Bigfoot's in Wisconsin.

At 5:20 p.m. on April 24, something like a kangaroo was even photographed near Waukesha, Wisconsin. Loren Coleman, to whom I'm indebted for collecting these reports, said the photo shows "a tan animal with lighter brown front limbs, hints of a lighter brown hind limb, dark brown or black patches around the eyes, inside the two upright ears, and possibly surrounding the nose and upper mouth area." He compares it favorably to Bennett's wallaby, or brush kangaroo, native to Tasmania, where the topography ranges from low valleys to snowy summits.[*]

Well, maybe and maybe not, according to Debbie Nelson, of the Kangaroo Conservation Center. Based in Dawsonville, Georgia, the center has the largest population of kangaroos in captivity, outside of Australia.

Of the reports printed here, she said, "Some of the 'kangaroo' sightings may have been wallabies [a small species of kangaroo]. They are becoming fairly common as pets all over the United States. These animals are known to escape from their owners from time to time. Some species are fairly hardy and may manage to survive for a time in the wild. We have been alerted before to kangaroo sightings in Georgia, and the animals were identified as wallabies that had escaped from private homes."

But it may not be as simple as that. Nelson said, "The tracks as described, if I understand them correctly, do not resemble the foot of a kangaroo."

If the truth is in the tracks, what is it? In each instance, whether called a werewolf, wallaby, Bigfoot, or kangaroo, I believe that what has been observed is the Chupacabras, or "goat-sucker," which was assumed to have made its mysterious debut in Puerto Rico in 1995. Since then it has been reported in Florida, Massachusetts, New York, New Jersey, Texas, and California. It is blamed for leaving a trail littered with dead livestock: eight sheep dead and drained of blood in Orocovis, Puerto Rico, in March 1995; caged rabbits "found dead with holes in the neck area, without a drop of blood" in Naguabo, Puerto Rico, on December 14, 1995; 69 goats, chickens, geese, and ducks killed in Sweetwater, Florida, in March 1996; a goat with three puncture marks on its neck, Rio Grande, Texas, in May 1996; and even an attack on a construction worker in Santa Ana, California, in June 1996.

The Chupacabras has been seen by various people, including Puerto Rican officials. As described, it reportedly attacks livestock, puncturing the animals' necks, suggesting that it may feed on the victim's blood. The marks are made by the upper teeth. There are no corresponding marks showing similar teeth on the lower jaw.

---

[*] The photo is reproduced in the book *The W-Files: True Reports of Unexplained Phenomena in Wisconsin.*

The odd thing is that until now there has been no established tradition of the Chupacabras. Things like lake monsters, Bigfoot, vampires, and so on all have long histories, which argue in favor of their realities; today's alien abduction is the night-visiting incubus of centuries ago. But the "Chupas," as it's nicknamed, seemed to come out of nowhere, giving rise to outrageous theories ranging from genetic experiments gone wrong to rampaging monsters off-loaded from flying saucers; the most outrageous theory is that Chupas was sent here by aliens to spread HIV.

To make matters more difficult, the description of Chupas varies with each witness. The first, best description came after six months of unexplained livestock mutilations in Puerto Rico. In September 1995, Madelyne Tolentino characterized it as a fanged kangaroo with bulging red eyes. Subsequent sightings offered more hysterical portraits. It was alternately described as having red feathers, gray fur, or scales—or all three. It is a mammal. Or it is a reptile, or an amphibian. It is upright and it has small arms and hands, and it has a muzzle. It has a long tail. It has pointed ears and large, wraparound eyes. In short, the best reports have it being kangaroo shape and kangaroo size. Its tracks show three toes, with webbed feet, and one report has it able to jump a 6-foot fence. And it does not walk or run. It *hops*.

As in Illinois, Chupas is sometimes called doglike. In Sweetwater, Florida, where it was seen in March 1996, it was "a dog-like figure standing up, with two short hands in the air." In June 1996, in the Sonora Desert of Mexico, it was "like a turkey or kangaroo." And in the Campo Rico district of Puerto Rico, it is not called Chupacabras at all but is referred to as *el canguro*.

If it is Chupacabras, we can understand the reaction of Police Officer Byrne and his partner when they faced the "growling," "vicious" creature in a dark Chicago alley back in 1974—the closest the predator has come to capture.

"Too bad we didn't have our nightsticks there," Byrne lamented. "Then we could have really hammered him."

CHAPTER 11
THE BLESSED VIRGIN IN THE LAND OF LINCOLN

The age of miracles has not passed. In America today, the Blessed Virgin Mary is at work, especially in Illinois. She is visiting the Chicago suburb of Hillside, and Belleville, near East St. Louis. These days she rides cars, hates drugs and abortion (no surprise), but is not above telling a good joke. After all, she says, her son "was not on His knees all the time."

Oh, and she's here because the world is ending—*soon.*

Even before the Bible was written, messengers from heaven came to earth. Greek and Roman gods were not above flirting (and more) with mortals, and in the Old Testament there was the pillar of fire and Ezekiel's wheel, with its strange many-headed beasts. Angels themselves came down, and of course so did God—to Moses. Similarly, the

Native American Ho-Chunk tribe encountered prophetic "shining be-ings" during their dream quests.

In the dawn of the Christian era, the first to come back was, of course, Christ, who after death stayed for 40 days among his as-tounded disciples. But since then it has primarily been his mother, Mary, who has made it her to duty to mix with mankind.

Mary does not figure in Jesus' trial and execution, though she does appear with the unnamed "beloved disciple" at the foot of the cross, to witness her child's fate. Two months later, in Jerusalem, she was in "the upper room," to pray with the disciples and 100 others. She was part of the core community that formed the Jerusalem church. During one of the meetings, according to the Book of Acts, she and her four sons then underwent a miraculous transformation. Tongues of fire filled them with the holy spirit. After that event, Mary is not mentioned in the Bible again.

Other sources have her join her son James in his work for the early church. One early tradition has her spend the next 22 years in Jerusalem, after which she is entombed in the Mount of Olives. Or she travels with John to Turkey, where they preach the gospel together un-til her death. The fifth-century manuscript "The Assumption of Mary" has her taken bodily into heaven, and so her remains have never been found.

Since the third century, Mary has made countless visitations. At Lourdes, France, on February 11, 1858, Bernadette Soubirous heard a noise like a tremendous storm while she was gathering firewood near a stream. From a cave or grotto came a golden cloud, which resolved into a beautiful woman who hovered above a bush. It was Mary, and she asked Soubirous to have a chapel built on the spot. As many as 20,000 attended later apparitions.

On May 13, 1917, Mary came to Fatima, Portugal, again as a rum-bling, powerful wind. Then appeared a gliding, white light, and in the light, Mary. She appeared to Lucia dos Santos, 10; Francisco Marto, 8; and Jacinto Marto, 7, who had been tending a flock of sheep. Subse-quent apparitions were attended by as many as 70,000.

Her appearances to six Croatian children in war-torn Bosnia in re-cent times have caused more than 11 million to come and witness her healing presence. One of the children, named Vicka, in 1987 met with Joseph Reinholtz, a retired railroad worker from Hillside, a suburb of Chicago. He had suffered from blurred vision and periods of blindness since September 1980. Vicka prayed over Reinholtz, and on his return to Illinois his sight gradually returned. The first thing he was able to see was a statue of Mary that he had bought years before; it was weeping!

Reinholtz returned to Medjugorje, Bosnia, in April 1989, and Vicka instructed him to look at home for a large crucifix next to a three-branched tree, where he was to pray. He later found the location at the Queen of Heaven Cemetery in Hillside. On August 15, 1990, Mary appeared to Reinholtz. She returned on November 1, 1990, with St. Michael and three other angels. The Virgin Mary now visits the cross daily, except Tuesdays. Coincidentally, Tuesdays are the days for which the Archdiocese of Chicago has placed a "restriction of obedience to the Church" on Reinholtz, asking him not to come to the cemetery.

St. Michael always comes with Mary, and sometimes St. Joseph and Jesus, do, too. Mortal visitors are said to have been able to photograph Mary, angels, and "light phenomena" at the site. Other phenomena include blood coming from the corpus on the cross, rosaries turned gold, and the scent of roses.

On the 25th of each month, Mary gives Reinholtz a message for the world. (See accompanying sidebar.)

At 3 a.m. on August 15, 1993, Mary took Reinholtz on a Dante-like tour of purgatory, which is distinct from Hell; it is a place where those who died in a state of grace can expiate their sins and be elevated to Heaven. Reinholtz recalled it as endless, "a gray area, dark like ashes, a somewhat very misty area." Purgatory was divided into three levels, with graduating severities of punishment. He could sense but not see the souls there, "begging and twitching for help."

Mary seems to like to travel. In October 1993, Joseph Reinholtz and a friend, Pat, were traveling to Michigan. Mary came along. Reinholtz recalled, "She had us laughing." The episode, outlined here, may seem bizarre to some, but I find it strangely reassuring—the Mother of God out for a little human fun.

"Two angels were in the backseat of the car, and Blessed Mary sat between Pat, driving, and me," Reinholtz said. "She said she wanted to see what it was like to ride in a car. I told Pat what Our Lady said, and we laughed so hard.

"Then Our Lady said, 'Joseph, I want Pat to open the doors to let us out.' I was still wiping the tears from laughing at her other sentence, and so I told Pat what Our Blessed Mother had said about her opening the car doors in Detroit, for her and the two angels. We laughed again.

MARY'S MESSAGE TO JOSEPH REINHOLTZ

Here is Mary's message to Joseph Reinholtz from June 25, 1996:

"Praise Jesus, praise Jesus, my children. Repent for your sins, my children, and convert yourselves to my Son, Jesus Christ.

"Dear children, some of you are still not praying the Rosary as I have asked. Pray, my children, with sincerity, reverence, love and devotion. Pray from your hearts, my children, so you can find the true peace and love that you desperately seek. I ask all of you to convert yourselves entirely to me as your heavenly Queen, the Mother of Peace. Please, my little children, continue to pray, pray for our Holy Father, the Pope, all my priests and deacons, brothers and nuns and laypersons so that they all continue to do God's work.

"Pray more, my children, for the sick and the elderly, and especially for the poor souls in Purgatory so that they can gain eternal rest in Heaven. I am your mother, the Queen of Peace and Queen of the most Holy Rosary, and I love you all and I bless you in the name of my Son, Jesus Christ. Go in peace, my children, and do good works. This is my request of you."

"Coming back, we rode with different angels and Blessed Mary in the car. At one point I looked [away], and Blessed Mary left. The two angels [were] with heads resting in hands against the windows. I looked across the seat, but she had left the angels alone with us. Then coming toward the car, in the sky, was Our Lady! Until she was on the hood.

"I said to Pat, 'Stop!' Because I see her so real, as a person, I was afraid she would be hit by traffic. And I began to scold her, and said, 'Don't frighten me like that. I love you too much.' Then Our Lady touched our rosaries and left us."

After Reinholtz suffered a stroke on February 10, 1995, Mary visited him in the hospital. He died in December 1996.

Ray Doiron, 63, first encountered the Blessed Virgin Mary on January 13, 1993, in Belleville. In an interview he is soft spoken and almost shy. Before his first visitation, Doiron had had three near-death experiences in his life and was deaf in his right ear. He had been sleeping on his living room couch, when he heard a soft voice.

"I opened my eyes to see this bright light, and in this bright light was a figure of a lady." The figure told Doiron to visit the nearby Lady of the Snows Shrine on February 11, and again on the 13th of the next three months. The 13th is a day that apparently has significance to Mary. When she had appeared to Lucia dos Santos at Fatima, it was, as Mary ordered, "for six successive months, on the 13th day at the same hour."

So on the eleventh, Doiron headed to the shrine, a replica of the one at Lourdes. It was cold and rainy, and after five minutes of prayer a strong wind came up. Then the wind stopped—and there was Mary. Her first message of many to Doiron was her shortest:

"Teach my people how to love my beloved Son, Jesus, with all their hearts. Teach people to love each other without jealous pride[*] or jealousy in their hearts. Work together with love for everyone. In order to have peace, it must first start in each person. All must pray, pray, pray for this, and peace will come!"

This simple message would become the basis for Mary's many later messages to Doiron, some of them lengthy and—if one may be excused for saying so—less organized. Through them all, Mary's call for all to "pray, pray, pray" was frequently repeated. Mary, whom Doiron would

---

[*] In Doiron's book, this passage was misprinted as "zealous pride." "Zeal doesn't have anything to do with it," he told me.

come to call "Little Lady," would later comment on a number of issues within the Catholic Church, including prayer in schools, abortion, and the separation of church and state.

At first, Mary asked Doiron to keep the messages secret.

"She did not want it to become a sideshow or carnival," Doiron wrote in a book outlining his experiences, *Messages from Our Heavenly Mother to Her Children,* which is in its third printing.

Mary's visits began to take on a pattern. There would be wind, which would stop. Gilding behind a statue at the shrine would turn blue. Then about 30 feet away there would be a bright light. From the light would emerge a "young and very regal" image of an impossibly beautiful woman. Usually she would be dressed in a white gown with a cowl, all of the apparition sparkling like diamonds, with glints of gold. Sometimes the cowl would be blue. Once she wore a crown, sort of a two-ringed halo with a dozen stars. Her hair was dark brown but her eyes, unexpectedly for a Middle Eastern Jew, were "very dark blue." Her voice was "soft and sweet, but with discipline." Doiron's sketches of Mary show her with hair parted in the middle, reaching down to her collar. Her forehead is somewhat high and broad, perhaps emphasized by her small chin. Her eyes are large and her lips are full. Doiron said Mary seemed to be between 18 and 25, and 5 feet 1 or 5 feet 2 inches tall.

Mary spoke to Doiron slowly and hesitatingly, so that he could memorize her words. "I try to write it down exactly as she tells me, but I know I will make mistakes in doing so," Doiron humbly confessed. "I know she will forgive me, because I am human."

Several times she brought along baby Jesus. The first was May 13, 1995, oddly enough the day before Mother's Day.

With permission, Doiron told a small number of friends, who began to attend the shrine with him. Then he was allowed to make the messages public. Doiron came to believe that his mission was to be the same as that of Paul, the Christians' tormentor who had been stricken by Christ, then told to spread the gospel throughout the ancient world. St. Paul's astounding travels, principally within Rome, led to Christianity's conquest of the Roman empire within just a few centuries of Christ's death and to the formation of the Catholic Church as we know it today.

"It must start with me first," Doiron wrote, "then my wife, my family, my friends, my church, and my community—and then the world!"

Before you question Doiron's concept of his duty, imagine how *you* would feel if you were absolutely convinced that God was speaking to

MARY'S MESSAGE TO RAY DOIRON

Here is one of Mary's briefer messages to Ray, in full, from April 13, 1993:

"You must go out into the wilderness and to the poor in spirit and preach a world-wide evangelism. God will minister miraculous healing during the time of world-wide evangelism.

"The Holy Spirit is the only Power on earth that can destroy the Power of Satan. He has given you, the believer, that power. This miraculous and supernatural power of God will be released for physical healing. All this healing will be under the dispensation of Grace.

"A mighty new anointing will come upon our wilderness and rivers of living water will burst forth that will produce streams and springs. It will be a mighty Baptism of the Holy Spirit. Just as the

Roman soldier pierced the side of Jesus on the cross, and water and blood flowed from his side, this is the way it will come. Jesus poured out the Holy Spirit to us in His death.

"As the anointing comes, you must respond because if you are not there to capture His touch, He may never pass you that way again.

"Remember, He does not follow you, you follow Him!

"You must learn to know and how to hear His voice when He calls. Just as Jesus said, 'My sheep hear My voice and I know them, and they follow Me.'

"You must desire to be with God to hear His voice, then you will feel the experience and experience His presence, power and love.

"Go in peace and love God!"

you regularly. In person Doiron is pleasant and retiring and claims no special wisdom. He prefers that his town of residence not be publicized, and he does not look forward to phone calls asking for prophecies. "As of the 13th of this month I'll have to carry a cell phone with me," he says. "I can't even go to the bathroom."

The apparitions eventually became public events attended by many. Over the months and years Mary set dates for her final appearance, and then kept appearing. But on November 13 and December 13, 1994, she did not appear at all. Doiron's wife was receiving radiation therapy at the time.

"This is my place at this time, with her," Doiron said.[*]

Mary had some tremendous revelations for Doiron, the greatest being that we are in fact in the Biblical period of Revelations: the final days. The stage has already been set and the signs are here, Mary said, including "the rise of one world government" and "the European Community."

But there were other, smaller revelations from Mary that, taken out of context, range from poetic to pedestrian and sometimes just blunt:

- On the clergy wearing street clothes: "I call upon my beloved priest-sons to examine their anointing and to wear their clerical collars and garb."
- On physical appearance: "I am beautiful because I love. If you want to be beautiful, love!"
- On parenting: "The youth today see adults using drugs, drunkenness, shootings, swearing, not going to church, cheating at their jobs, and taking of the life of a child in the mother's womb through abortion. This is plain murder!!"
- On abortion: "[M]y tiniest dear children are killed in their mother's wombs every day, more than all of these past wars put together. (...) My little children, put to death all of these things that lead you way from God..."
- On politics: "The West had made civilization progress, but without God, as if they were their own creator. This is wrong. Look at Russia."

---

[*] Mary was not always so open to compromise. On February 11, 1998, Doiron asked Mary to make it stop raining until after the apparition. She refused, calling the rain "a reminder of the many tears I have shed for this world."

And my next-to-favorite comment: "When people try to play God, they are in serious trouble."

But my favorite revelation was this look at the importance of humor: "My Son Jesus tried to develop a deeper spiritual feeling in the heart of his flock, but He also enjoyed His keen and quiet sense of humor and encouraged the laughter in the most serious talks on spirituality. Do you think My Son Jesus ever laughed? He did. He was not on His knees all the time."

I like this vision of a laughing Jesus, but sadly, Mary of late has had Armageddon on her mind. On August 13, 1998, she warned that "those who do not listen to my followers and messages I give, will fall under me into the fires of hell." She added, "You are living in the century controlled by Satan, that is coming to an end."

What it all boils down to is not complex. Doiron told me that "it's all very simple. She's warning us. Just the way your mother would."

During her last appearance before the completion of this book's manuscript, on February 11, 1999, she promised only one more public visit to the shrine—ever. It was to have occurred May 13, 1999. In her February message, she made vague references to the new millennium and to the pending martyrdom of clergy alive today. It seems clear that the end is very, very close.

Or is it? As Doiron himself wrote, "I don't know what this sounds like to someone else reading this. Maybe it doesn't make any sense to them. I don't know if I could believe it either if someone told me this, but I know in my heart that all of this took place."

So how does it feel to have been chosen as Mary's missionary? "You cry a lot," Doiron told me. "It's sad, you know? Like a death."

It is easy for even the devout to be skeptical when it comes to apparitions of the Blessed Virgin Mary. But I do wonder why it is that so many of us are at least willing to stop and consider the possibilities of flying saucers, ghosts, and Bigfoot, for example, while at the same time giggling over the possibility of God.

In the end, I think one of Doiron's perspectives is the best way to frame the experience, whatever one's beliefs:

"We hear of a place where Our Lady is appearing, and we go there at all cost. Then we hear of another place and we run to that at all cost. Then we hear of another place and we run to that place. Our Lady is appearing all over the United States today. We do not need to chase

OTHER APPEARANCES OF THE BLESSED VIRGIN

Obviously it is not for the sake of Illinois alone that the Virgin Mary frequently returns to earth. In May 1998, she caused her image to appear between the double panes of a glass freezer door at a grocery in Jersey City, New Jersey. The silhouette of a hood-wearing woman lasted four days, during which time hundreds of the faithful offered up candles, messages, and flowers.

Mary's image had similarly appeared a year to the month earlier, in Estill Springs, Tennessee. The church, as is so often the case, was slow to recognize the miracle. Said one cleric, "When the good Lord comes, he won't come on a major appliance."

In 1993 80,000 worshipers gathered at the farm of Nancy Fowler, near Conyers, Georgia, where the Virgin Mary had appeared annually since 1983. Crowds had steadily grown over the years to the point that in 1992, a traffic jam of the faithful outside the farm prevented emergency workers from reaching a woman with heart problems. Attendance in 1998 had dropped to a mere 30,000. The Virgin announced then, through Fowler, that this would be her last visit.

Though only Fowler was ever able to actually see and hear the Virgin Mary, some attendants to the miracles said that the sun changed color during the communions, and some smelled roses.

Though the Virgin will no longer visit the farm, there is still a well on the property, which Jesus himself blessed—a welcome relief to weary pilgrims. In 1991, the Rockdale County Health Department asked Nancy Fowler to post the well, warning that it had tested positive for unsafe levels of coliform bacteria.

rainbows, looking for a pot of gold. Our rainbow is wherever you are. Be with the people of your family and friends and pray together.

"Your rainbow is in your everyday life."

(Ray Doiron's book, "Messages from Our Heavenly Mother to Her Children," is available for $6 from The People's Prayer Group, P.O. Box 14, Breese, IL 62230. Profits go to the Catholic Urban Program.)

CHAPTER 12
ATLANTIS IN ILLINOIS?

Cahokia Mounds State Historic Site is all that remains of the Western Hemisphere's most sophisticated prehistoric civilization north of Mexico. It is eight miles from St. Louis, near Collinsville, and covers 2,200 acres.

Cahokia is a place of mystery, built by an unknown white race that practiced cannibalism while the pharaohs ruled Egypt. Their origin is unknown. And they fled their complex city for no known reason.

Author and amateur archaeologist Frank Joseph believes that Cahokia was an outpost of Atlantis. After leaving Cahokia, he maintains, the prehistoric people traveled south and founded the Aztec civilization. Believe it or not, I agree.

The established facts are strange enough. Cahokia was a late settlement for these strange people, built around 700. At its peak, from 1100 to 1200 A.D., the city was the capital of the far-flung mound-building Mississippian culture, which for 4,100 years had *already* extended to both coasts. The city proper covered nearly six square miles, with houses laid out on a grid, European-style. Outside the city were farms.

Before Cahokia, beginning in 3000 B.C., the Mississippian culture fielded expeditions to Michigan, where tremendous amounts of copper were mined, and then shipped, from enormous stone piers for trade throughout the continent—and perhaps beyond.

Then, in 1400 A.D., Cahokia's makers abandoned its mines, outposts, and magnificent city. They simply disappeared.

It's possible that some of the Cahokians became what later explorers knew as the Mandan Indians of Minnesota and the Dakotas. The Mandans themselves are something of a puzzle. Captain Pierre La Verendrye, visiting a Mandan tribe in 1738, noted that their village was laid out similarly to Cahokia, though that abandoned capital had yet to be rediscovered. The Mandans' villages had blocks and streets. They lived inside a stockaded fort, surrounded by moat. As for the Mandans themselves, "This nation is mixed white and black," he wrote. "The women are fairly good-looking, especially the white, many with blond and fair hair."

Many suggestions have been made as to the reason for Cahokia's abandonment. Some blame depletion of natural resources; others blame a change of climate sometime after 1200 A.D. Other possibilities include war, disease, and even "social unrest."

Originally, Cahokia had been surrounded by a two-mile stockade constructed from 15,000 to 20,000 oak and hickory logs, each a foot in diameter and 20 feet tall. The walls were probably covered in clay. This habit of building fortress-communities is unique to the Mississippian culture.

The advanced state of Cahokian civilization was revealed in the early 1960s when Dr. Warren Wittry revealed numerous large oval-shaped pits, which seemed to be arranged in arcs of circles. Wittry believed that that complex arrangement served as a calendar, which he dubbed "Woodhenge." Solstices and equinoxes could have been predicted using Woodhenge, and there are indications that suggest that eclipses could have been predicted as well. Some alignments suggest that the moon and certain stars had significance to the Cahokians.

The largest mound at Cahokia—in fact, the largest man-made earthen mound in the North American continent—is Monks Mound, named for a group of Trappist monks who once lived nearby. It is estimated that the weathered mound originally roughly measured 955 by

Cahokia's Monks Mound today, the largest known man-made earthen mound in North America. Was it an outpost of fabled Atlantis? Its builders' origin and fate are still in dispute. Courtesy Cahokia Mounds State Historic Site.

774 feet and was 92 feet high, though it could have been larger. It is one of the few terraced mounds in North America, with two plateaus as it ascends; it originally probably had four. It strikingly suggests the shape of the Aztec pyramids, which would be built later.

Cahokia's name comes not from its builders but from a subtribe of the Illini, the Cahokia, who occupied the area when French explorers arrived. Native Americans met by settlers near a similar Cahokian fortress-settlement in Wisconsin, at Aztalan, told strange stories of the Cahokians: their hair was like fire, their eyes like ice, and some of the men had faces like bears. The Antewandetton Indians who once lived near the Great Lakes said the Cahokians were "white people." The Menomonie recalled that they had light skin. When presented with one of Cahokia's copper artifacts when it was excavated in the late 18th century, an Ojibwa elder responded, "White man make long ago, way back."

Scientists call the Cahokians "Archaeo-Indians." The later Wood-land Indians called them "Marine Men." The Marine Men called them-selves Tirajana. Whoever they were, they removed more than 500,000 tons of copper from Michigan's Upper Peninsula. There were 5,000 in-dividual mines, each four to seven miles long, together peppering three

Michigan counties. If all the mines in just one of the counties were placed end to end, they would form a trench five miles long, 20 feet wide, and 30 feet deep.

An estimated 10,000 laborers toiled there for more than a thousand years; the erection of Cahokia was a late achievement for these people. In Michigan, huge stone wharves survive, testimony to their reputation among the native Indians as "Marine Men." The mines themselves were outfitted with implements of every imaginable type, some of them of massive size. One of the gigantic copper ore nuggets found in one of the surviving wooden cribs at the mines weighed six tons. It is now housed at the Smithsonian Institution.

The ore was shipped south to Aztalan, at Rock Lake, Wisconsin, where it was processed. Where such a tremendous amount of copper went after that remains an archaeological question.

At the same time, Europe was enjoying its Bronze Age. Bronze is made of copper and tin. One of the great archaeological mysteries of Europe has been where all the necessary copper came from. Known, workable, mixed-quality deposits in Great Britain and Spain would have been quickly exhausted.

James Scherz, professor of civil engineering at the University of Wisconsin, summed up the twin mysteries. "One of the basic questions that hasn't been basically answered yet is, where did all the copper from Lake Superior go? All of the copper found in the mounds, although a large amount, is but a small percentage of that mined. The Europeans have a complementary problem. Where did all their copper come from? The Europeans were in a copper-trading frenzy from 2000 to 1000 B.C., like we are about oil now, because copper drove their economy."

Coincidence? It gets stranger.

For shipment throughout the Mediterranean, copper was cast in a very peculiar shape, which allowed it to be handled easily. The shape of the ingot was called an "ox hide," as it roughly resembled the hide of an ox. It was a square with concave sides, with legs sticking from each corner for easy handling. Bronze Age shipping vessels have been excavated in the Mediterranean, yielding many such ingots. The peculiar shape became something of an icon and was even retained for smaller ingots, used as money. Besides the Mediterranean, ox hide ingots have been recovered from archaeological sites in western Mexico and from Michigan's Upper Peninsula. You can see one in the Michigan State Museum at Lansing.

But how could the Cahokians be responsible for global copper trade at such an early period? Such a feat would be within the capability of only the most incredible ancient cultures, such as—oh—the fabled Atlantis.

And, in fact, Atlantis was reigning supreme at this period, enjoying great wealth derived from its trade throughout the known world of precious metals, especially "orichalch." So abundant was Atlantis's supply of orichalch that its citizens even built long walls of it, delineating the borders of their states. Today we call orichalch copper.

The Mississippian culture's mines in the Upper Peninsula closed precisely when Europe's Bronze Age ended; the Bronze Age was not supplanted by the Iron Age—instead, Europe stagnated. Coincidentally, or perhaps not, the Bronze Age ended when Atlantis supposedly sank.

But was Atlantis real? It probably was, but we have to realize that our image of it probably differs from fact. What we know about the lost civilization comes from two accounts written by Plato (427 to 347 b.c.) and from possible references in the Bible. Before Plato, the historian Marcellus recorded ancestral legends about Atlantis. While the original text has been lost, commentaries on Marcellus's work have survived.

Plato wrote that Atlantis was a place named for and ruled by Atlas. Spiritually, then, it was the center of the earth. And it was probably the center in commercial and governmental terms as well. There was a central island, at the edge of the known world. That places it somewhere outside the Mediterranean but not necessarily that far into the Atlantic. Surrounding the main island were two zones of land and two zones of water, all of which were Atlantean territory. Ten kings governed the empire independently, but all were bound by a sort of common constitution, and they were surprisingly liberal.

Atlantis enjoyed tremendous natural resources. The Atlanteans were expert miners, domesticators of animals, and builders. They constructed palaces, temples, and docks and joined their regions with a network of canals. They were huge consumers of copper and gold. Thanks to their expert sailors, they exploited trade opportunities throughout the known world.

And then they passed beneath the sea. The Egyptian priests who told the story to Solon made the disaster into a moral: Atlantis perished because of its "overweening pride." Similarly, many have long

A diorama created by Lloyd K. Townsend showing Cahokia at its peak, in 1100 A.D. Note the Aztec-style pyramid, constructed by Cahokia's "white-skinned" cannibal artisans. Courtesy Cahokia Mounds State Historic Site.

taken Plato's rambling account to be a parable, a myth made up to teach a lesson.

If so, Plato failed. His accounts do have symbolism but are more like confusing and contradictory historical fact than clear prose. He teaches no lesson and there is none to be learned. So is it journalism?

Plato's knowledge was thirdhand. In his native Greece, the story was probably folklore, with too few details for the extended descriptions Plato provided. Those details he credited to Solon, who learned the larger story in Egypt. Solon passed the legend to Dropidas, a relative of Plato's, who then passed it to Critias the elder, then to Callaeschrus, then to Dropidas, then to Critias the younger, and finally to the latter's nephew, Plato.

Given the story's lengthy provenance, it is hardly surprising that Plato got Atlantis's age wrong. He placed the island's destruction in 14,000 B.C., a time in which it is hard to imagine civilization at all, let alone one of Atlantis's reputed superiority. It is also difficult to believe that the Atlantis legend would have survived that long merely as an oral tradition, no matter how famous it once had been.

But Plato was going from the Egyptian legend, and the Egyptians were on a lunar calendar. The Greeks were on a solar one. Corrected, the date of Atlantis's destruction moves ahead in time to 1200 B.C. Assuming that that date is rough, we can then look with more than a little interest at the geologic record. A massive volcano erupted on the island of Santorini in 1500 B.C., which devastated the Mediterranean and literally buried Minoan civilization—which may have been part of At-

An artist's diorama by William R. Iseminger, suggesting Cahokia between 1100 and 1150 A.D., when it was the sprawling, stockaded capital of the far-flung and mysterious Mississippian culture. Courtesy Cahokia Mounds State Historic Site.

lantis; this far back, names given millennia later by scientists mean nothing and become frustratingly changeable.

That such a story could survive 700 or 800 years until finally recorded by Plato is fairly reasonable, if such a place actually existed.

Using journalism's rules, we can at least look for confirmation of the Atlanteans' actions, if not their existence. If there were an Atlantis, and if it were overwhelmed by a natural disaster, it follows that its survivors became refugees. Now the researcher begins to get lucky, as this is the point when recorded history begins. Stories are written down.

Dates still are murky, but in the last third of the 14th century B.C., a volcanic eruption was observed. It was a disaster of Biblical proportions—literally. This is from the Old Testament (Exodus 12:28). Soon after, a "People of the Sea" did come to Libya, where they formed an alliance and joined in war against Egypt. The People of the Sea lost, were captured, and were offered resettlement in Egypt. They accepted, and flourished.

But there were other People of the Sea still searching for a new home. Some made their way to Syria, where they again formed an alliance and attacked Egypt. Again, they were captured, were killed, or resettled. The Sea People were scattered and incorporated into the cultures whose written histories are among the first we have.

Frank Joseph's theory is that the Atlanteans founded an American Midwestern outpost, mined copper, cast it into ingots, and shipped it back, fueling Europe's Bronze Age. A cataclysm destroyed Atlantis, and survivors in the Wisconsin settlement closed shop and migrated south. After a while they came back, founded Cahokia and Aztalan, and re-opened the mines. Then they left once more, created a new Aztalan in Mexico, and became the Aztecs. The Aztecs themselves referred to their far-away, long-ago homeland—wherever it was—as "Aztlan," and one of their legends recalled the fate of their relatives there: "They were swallowed by the waters and their souls became fish. The heavens collapsed upon them and in a single day they perished. All the mountains perished."

In all, there is nothing unreasonable about the theory that Atlantis was real and that its knowledge of shipping was so advanced that its empire spanned the globe. There are enough islands, and there may have been more, to provide way stations along the necessary routes. It is possible. But possibility is not proof.

Whatever Cahokia's true origins are, it is significant all by itself. In 1982 the United Nations Educational, Scientific, and Cultural Organization designated Cahokia Mounds a World Heritage Site for its importance to our understanding of the prehistory of North America.

Cahokia Mounds is managed by the Illinois Historic Preservation Agency. It is open daily. Admission is free, though a donation of $2 for adults and $1 for children is suggested.

CHAPTER 13
LAKE MICHIGAN

S erpents, disappearing planes, and ghostly Christmas ships—
Lake Michigan is big enough to contain many mysteries.

It is the third largest of the Great Lakes, the sixth-largest lake in the world: 307 miles long, 118 miles wide, and 22,400 square miles. The lake, at its deepest, is 923 feet. It was discovered by Europeans in 1634 by Jean Nicolet. It connects, via the Chicago Sanitary and Ship Canal, to the Mississippi River, and by the river to the Gulf of Mexico. Its only natural outlet is Lake Huron. Through lake Michigan runs a magnetic anomaly called an "isogonic line," which continues southeast.

Magnetic north, read by compasses, seldom points to true north, the direction of the pole. But along an isogonic line it does, simplifying the tasks of chart makers and navigators. This particular line is called the "agonic line."

We don't need to look to the supernatural to find the bizarre on Lake Michigan. On June 26, 1954, a tremendous wave came from nowhere and smashed into Chicago, killing seven. The wave reached 8 feet at the city's Montrose Harbor and 10 feet at North Avenue. This was an example of the Great Lakes' "seiche wave," an unexpected wall of water driven perhaps by faraway storms.

Some of the lake's other mysteries are also undoubtedly of this world but no less strange for that: water creatures, long known to Native Americans before white settlement. The prehistoric mound builders of Cahokia and Aztalan—whoever they were—built effigy mounds in their honor. The later Woodland Indians made offerings to the beasts, sprinkling tobacco on the waters. The creatures were variously called "Wak Tcexi" or "Winnebozho" by the Ho-Chunk Indians, and "Lenapizha" by the Peoria Indians.

The Lenapizha had real actions; they were said to have long tails and evil moods, sometimes overturning Indian canoes, drowning the natives. At night, so went the legends, the creatures would climb the banks and come ashore. In the Indian pantheon, these were evil spirits, who frequently battled with benign Thunderbirds.

On Lake Michigan, the earliest sightings of Lenapizha by whites were made in August 1867. The crews of two boats, the *George W. Wood* and the *Sky Lark*, said that they saw a serpentine creature off Evanston. A fisherman named Joseph Muhike later saw it a mile and a half off Chicago's Hyde Park.

By the turn of the century, the creature seemed to have moved north along Lake Michigan's shore, to Milwaukee, where "a ferocious looking beast" was sighted by commercial fisherman. Boaters in the city's bay were similarly surprised when they soon afterward saw what appeared to be "a large cask" floating near their boat. "When they passed near it they saw that it was the head of a large serpentine animal which was floating at rest," wrote historian Charles Brown.

Brown also collected one of the strangest stories ever to come out of the lake: a Native American Ojibwa legend of a lost land with very strange natives. Set sometime in the 1700s, it tells of an island tribe of Bigfoot, which the Ojibwa called "Windigo":

"Four Indian families left their camp for the summer. They made a big boat with a sail. They sailed for a long time and finally reached an island, where they landed. When they left the boat, a large number of Windigos came and wished to kill them. But the Windigos gave them rings and brooches and made friends with them. They [the Windigos] killed a deer and gave it to the Indians. The Indians lived on the island a long time.

"One day they saw a ship. They waved a blanket and it came to the island. The Windigos were sorry to see the Indians leave. They wanted to get into the ship, but the white men on the ship were afraid of them. But for the gifts, the Windigos would have killed and eaten the Indians."

As strange as the tale seems, modern stories are even stranger. These are the lake's mysteries that hint at forces beyond human comprehension, that exact a price in human life—forces perhaps beyond earth. There are more unexplained disappearances of aircraft and ships in the Great Lakes than in any other body of water in the world, including the Bermuda Triangle.* This chapter reports just a fraction of them.

The most recent disappearance was to the north, on the night of December 11, 1998. The 42-foot commercial fishing boat *Linda E* had left Milwaukee for Port Washington. It was equipped with a radio and cellular phone. The weather was not good, but it was not bad, either: winds from the east at 10 to 15 knots, up to 18 knots the next morning. At 9:45 p.m. the crew sent out a standard message to Port Washington. There was no word of distress. And there was never again word from the *Linda E*. Six miles from shore, it vanished. No sign of its wreckage, crew, or cargo was found after two and a half days of searching. Amy Gaskill, of the Coast Guard, announced, "This is one of those *X-Files* kinds of cases. It's mind boggling."

The Coast Guard, U.S. and Canadian Air Forces, commercial fishermen, and the Wisconsin Department of Natural Resources had searched 3,000 square miles of Michigan, an area three times the size of Rhode Island.

"Usually there is debris or something floating on the water to give us an indication that the ship went down, or we hear from the people we are looking for," Gaskill said. But there was no sign of the boat's foundering—no indication that it sank at all. Missing are Captain Leif Weborg, 55; Warren Olson, 45; and Scott Matta, 32. They left behind family and friends.

Unfortunately the *Linda E* isn't unique. She's just recent. Author Jay Gourley, in his outstanding book *The Great Lakes Triangle*, identifies one spot where losses occur with astounding frequency. It is the

---

* It may be a coincidence, but the same isogonic line that runs through Lake Michigan continues to the southwest, where it passes through the Bermuda Triangle. In both areas, navigation should therefore be easier, not more difficult. At any rate, I find the Bermuda Triangle's reputation to be vastly exaggerated.

relatively small area east of a line between Chicago and Milwaukee. In this area, planes and ships seem to vanish, sometimes reappearing to astonished onlookers. At other times, navigational instruments seem to relay impossible information. And in some instances, experienced sailors and fliers seem to behave in ways that could be explained only by insanity.

But losses occur all over the lake, not just in this one area. In the spring of 1872, the schooner *George F. Whitney* was lost and presumed foundered in the middle of Lake Michigan. None of her crew of eight was ever found, nor was the ship. Before the trip, at dock in Chicago, Captain Carpenter had displayed all his flags at half-mast, with the American flag upside down—a universal symbol of distress. When asked why he had done so, Captain Carpenter responded, strangely, that it was an invitation to tugs to take him upriver.

The *Alpena* was a freight and passenger ship. As late as 3 a.m. on October 16, 1880, she was seen by the schooner *Challenger* steaming full speed toward Chicago, just 35 miles away; strangely, she should already have arrived. *Alpena* had left Grand Haven, Michigan, for her nightly run at 10 p.m., carrying between 60 and 100 passengers and crew. Her sister ship had passed her at the midway point at 1 a.m. By morning *Alpena* was steaming away from her destination and was trailing the barge *S. A. Irish,* which was being towed to Milwaukee. *Alpena* was far off course. At noon the ship was traveling in tandem with the schooner *Grand Haven,* just five miles from Racine, Wisconsin, south of Milwaukee. *Alpena* turned and headed toward the middle of the lake. She was next seen northeast of Racine by the schooner *Levi Grant.* Her wheels were turning, her whistle was sounding, and steam was observed to be coming from the engines' scape pipes. But the crew of the *Levi Grant,* just a mile and a half away, could see no smoke coming from her stacks; there could have been no fire under the boilers. *Alpena* was never seen again. There were no signs of wreckage and no survivors.

Similarly, the *William B. Davoc* disappeared somewhere in the lake on November 11, 1940. This was no schooner but a huge coal carrier bound for south Chicago. She entered the lake at noon and is presumed to have collided with the 2,280-ton steamer *Anna C. Minch,* only because half of the steamer was found adrift. She'd been sheared in two, and there were no survivors. The other half, and the *William B. Davoc,* were never found. Neither ship had issued distress calls.

Changing technologies brought changing losses. On August 26, 1953, United Airlines flight 314 took off from Chicago's Midway Airport for Cleveland. It was 6:58 p.m. The pilot was Captain Lewis M. Brubaker, 32. Two minutes later, American Airlines flight 714 took off from Midway, piloted by Captain Dwight W. Davison. It was headed to Ypsilanti, Michigan. The pilots and copilots of both planes had thousands of hours of experience. There was a full bright moon, and the sky was clear. Visibility was unlimited. At one point, however, Captain Brubaker glanced down at his controls, and when he looked back up there was American 714, full in his windshield. At 10,800 feet, in the southeast corner of Lake Michigan, the planes collided. American 714 returned to Midway, and United 314 limped along to South Bend, Indiana. The Civil Aeronautics Board's only concise observation was that "[a]ll of the pilots should have been able to see the other aircraft [well before the crash]." But they hadn't.

The next day, on August 27, 1953, Air Force pilot John William Wilson was flying an F-86 at 15,000 feet over southern Lake Michigan. Just 500 feet behind him was another F-86, piloted by Lieutenant Goll Garrett. On an F-86, the radio microphone is in place in front of the pilot, and all a pilot has to do to transmit is to press a button on the control stick. Garrett tells the story: "I heard Wilson call base saying there was an emergency and indicating he would bail out. But almost as he spoke the plane flew apart. No parachute was seen, and I believe Wilson never got out of his seat." No trace of the plane or pilot was ever found.

An experienced commercial pilot was at the controls of a Piper PA-23, N4596P, when it flew toward Chicago's Meigs Field on November 29, 1960. There were two passengers. Just before landing, the pilot leveled off at 100 feet and told the tower he would "go around" and try again. This in itself is not unusual. But the pilot then turned right, away from downtown, and out toward Lake Michigan. Air traffic controllers watched as N4596P disappeared into a "snowy cloud." That was the last anyone saw or heard from the flight.

On February 6, 1961, a large number of UFO reports were made across the country—The Chicago Tribune itself reported many the next day. Also that night, Peter Dekeita, 29, pushed the control yoke all the way forward and dove his Viscount PA-22 at full throttle into ice on Lake Michigan, just four miles from Meigs Field. He had 5,000 hours of experience. The weather was perfect. He was just on Chicago's shore when he told Joliet Radio, "Having trouble, going into lake." Asked what the nature of his trouble was, he merely repeated, "Having trouble, going into lake."

The wreckage was recovered. Investigation showed that the airplane had been building speed at the time of the crash. The engine and controls were all fine. The only possible explanation was suicide, but a check of Dekeita's background ruled this out.

Other incidents also reveal wreckage but no reason for the tragedy. In the Chicago suburb of Markham, on September 6, 1964, a twin-engine Piper PA-23, N1252P, crashed, killing the pilot, a friend, and the friend's wife. All were pilots. After taking off from Howell Airport, witnesses later said, the plane sounded as if one engine were being raced. The plane dropped its landing gear, turned, and slowed. Investigation showed that both engines were fine, right to the point of impact, which happened within sight of the airport. There had been no malfunction.

Robert Anderson had more than 4,000 hours as a commercial pilot. On December 1, 1964, he was flying a Piper PA-30, N7057Y, from Meigs Field to Terre Haute, Indiana. The weather was good. He had one passenger. After takeoff he had been cleared to climb to 3,000 feet and turn eastward over Lake Michigan. But just two minutes after leaving the ground, according to the captain of the tug *Annie G*, Anderson was flying at high speed only 10 feet above the water. The plane crashed. No wreckage was ever found, nor was Anderson, though searchers went directly to the spot. The passenger washed ashore three months later.

On August 16, 1965, at three seconds past 9:20 p.m., the pilot of United Airlines flight 389 calmly reported that he was checking his altimeter. Yet the Boeing 727 was seconds away from the surface of Lake Michigan. Captain Melville Towle, 42; his flight engineer, Maurice Femmer, 26; and copilot Roger Whitezell had a combined total of 26,000 hours of flight experience. They didn't have to check the altimeter; they could have just looked out the window to see Lake Michigan rushing up at them at 2,000 feet per minute. The crew, three stewardesses, and 28 passengers all died.

United 389 had not stopped to level off after descending, as told to by Chicago Center, through 6,000 feet. At that point, United 389 was just 40 miles from Chicago. It crashed within sight of the city three minutes later, just 20 miles distant. The fireball, from shore, seemed to cover the entire sky.

The National Transportation Safety Board concluded, "No reasonable explanation for [the crew's] failure to level the aircraft at 6,000 feet, their assigned altitude, can be offered. This is particularly true when one considers the fact that the last communication from the flight which ended at 2120:03 made reference to the altimeter setting."

The U.S. Air Force's North American Air Defense Command (NORAD), consulted by the Transportation Safety Board, reported that it had a clear recorded track of United 389. It also had another clear track, of another object; both were assumed to show United 389, since it was the only flight in the area and since one track disappeared three minutes before the accident and the other appeared two minutes before. Unfortunately, this last track continued at 390 miles per hour—above the speed of sound—for two minutes *after* the crash, to a point 23 miles west of where the wreckage was discovered. Air Traffic Control decided that the NORAD data must have been erroneous.

Joan Williams, 39, flew her Cessna 170B, N2522C, from Chicago's Wings Airport at noon on March 20, 1965. She had fuel for four and a half hours. She and the plane were never seen again.

On March 8, 1968, James Looker was flying a DeHavilland Dove, N999NJ. He was carrying a family of five. Looker was a former test pilot with Piper Aircraft, and he had 10,000 hours of flying experience. His plane had sophisticated instrumentation that should have been able to fly the plane down to the runway. At 7:50 p.m. he sent a strange call to Chicago, indicating that he was fighting a 45- to 50-knot headwind. But the airport knew that on the ground there was only a mild breeze, and that should have been a tailwind for Looker. Weather balloons released by the airport confirmed this. Looker was 20 miles from the east shore of Lake Michigan when N999NJ disappeared from Chicago Center radar. Not only could radar not pick up the plane, it could not pick up the plane's radar beacon or transponder. Advised of this, Looker couldn't explain it, but he reported his altitude and position verbally. Twelve minutes later, Looker was within unpowered gliding distance of Meigs Field, just a few miles to the east. Meigs Tower gave Looker clearance to land. He never did, nor did he respond to radioed queries. The Coast Guard conducted visual and dragging searches but could find no trace of the plane or its occupants.

Just north of Chicago, at Grayslake, a 29-year-old flight instructor took off in a Piper-28, N6678W, on June 17, 1969. The pilot had more than 1,000 flight hours in just such a plane, 100 of them probably spent teaching students how to handle stalls. So why the pilot stalled N6678W and immediately shot into the ground is inexplicable. The official determination: "Miscellaneous: power plant failure for undetermined reason." The pilot lived for ten more days and did not or could not explain what had happened.

On July 21, 1972, Anderson Duggar, Jr., was 15 miles east of Milwaukee in a Piper PA-31, N212AD. He had more than 4,000 hours of experience. Weather was excellent. At 9:10 a.m. Milwaukee Approach radar watched Duggar disappear from radar. Despite an extensive search, no trace was ever found of the plane, or Duggar, again. The accident investigation could say only that "it is presumed that the aircraft crashed."

A few months later, Lawrence Nelms, 50, a pilot with 21,000 hours of experience, was flying a Beech Expeditor 3TM from Detroit to Milwaukee. The weather was good, so he was flying visually. Because of that, his flight was not tracked by Detroit. It never arrived. No distress call was made. Not a scrap of wreckage was ever found.

A few months later yet, on December 27, James Rose, 47, was flying from Moline to Northbrook, just north of Chicago. He had been a pilot for 13 years. At 8:20 p.m., however, Milwaukee Radio noted that he was far off course, near Janesville, Wisconsin. Milwaukee Radio had Rose relay the readings from his navigational radios and gave him a course to Northbrook. They then had Rose confirm each detail of the instructions. According to the instruments, Rose was now on course and should have been well within range of Chicago Radio. But he couldn't make contact, and Milwaukee heard his signal fade as the pilot should have neared Chicago. Chicago never picked up Rose. The Civil Air Patrol searched but found nothing. Some parts that could have come from his plane did wash ashore near Milwaukee later, but they were too close; Milwaukee had heard Rose's signal fade away. More incredibly, how could Rose have flown out over Lake Michigan without knowing he was flying away from Northbrook? The National Transport Safety Board could say only that Rose's fate was "presumed" to have been a crash.

Professional pilot John J. Fair was flying an Aerostar 601 on the morning of October 3, 1973. Fair had more than 6,000 hours of flying experience, and the plane was well regarded for its responsive controls. Fair's flight plan called for him to fly on instruments until he could see Chicago's Meigs Field, when he would fly visually. A minute from the airport, two miles from the runway, he dove into Lake Michigan. So great was his speed that the gas in the wing tanks exploded. Investigators found that the plane was in fully controlled flight when it crashed.

For the last, I have saved the most famous of all the ship disappearances on Lake Michigan, that of Chicago's "Christmas ship," the *Rouse Simmons*.

She left Thompson Harbor, southwest of Manistique, Michigan, at noon on November 25, 1913, with her annual load of Christmas trees for Chicago. Captain Herman Schunemann had sent word that he would arrive early on the 27th. But at noon on the 26th the schooner was spotted on the eastern shore, at the Lifesaving Service Station at Sturgeon Bay, Wisconsin. The *Rouse Simmons* was making excellent time but was flying distress pennants. Too late to reach the speedy ship, Sturgeon Bay station notified Kewaunee station, 25 miles to the south, and crews there set out in large boats to try to meet her. They spotted the schooner and then watched as a veil of thick mist blotted her out. The lifesaving crews carried on but could not find the *Rouse Simmons*. Long overdue, her crew of 17 was presumed lost. Only the captain's wallet was recovered, ten years later, in the nets of commercial fishermen.

But the ship sailed on—or so some said. She was spotted by "patrols and sentries" on the morning of December 21, 1917, and again on August 19, 1919, when the "hulk of an ancient ship" was seen by the *S. S. Carolina* a few miles from Chicago.

The Coast Guard tried to follow up on the sighting but could see nothing in the heavy mist. Anyway, Coast Guard Captain John Anderson called the story "impossible."

But even if the story isn't true, it is so perfect and poetic that I wish the sightings had continued. I would like very much to see a speedy, misty Christmas ship, one whose distress has long since passed. And so I place her in my special folder of unexplained tales. It's a slim file, otherwise reserved for jolly spirits, like those that would have attended *Rouse Simmons's* cargo on her arrival in Chicago: tales that *should* be true. And that therefore *are*.

CHAPTER 14
VAMPIRES, GIANT BIRDS, CROP CIRCLES, AND OTHER ODDS AND ENDS

One story about a strange, hairy creature on two legs is a mystery to be avoided late in the evening. The strangeness, the inexplicable and unheard-of details thrill the reader and make you clutch the quilt a little tighter around your neck at night. It's quiet, so quiet, *too* quiet. And after a while you don't *want* it to be so quiet because you are listening so hard without meaning to, and the contrast of a scratch at your window will stand out all the more. And you certainly won't look out!

When I was young and visiting my grandparents, late at night I was afraid to look in the guest-room mirror, for fear of seeing the image of the dead great-aunt whose room it had been before she died at 13. Years later I found out my sister had the same fear.

On the other hand, 20 sightings of Bigfoot, or UFOs, or ghosts are, well…as the patterns emerge, as the consistency of the reports becomes obvious, just as these things are seen likely to be—some of the mystery drops away. We are beginning to put our mysteries in tidy, nonthreatening categories.

So how much more horrible is the isolated event—the encounter that was never repeated, the one-shot terror or handful of sightings that are the most inexplicable of the unexplained? These we cannot call science or even journalism. They are only legend.

In what category, for example, can we place this tale of Devil's Bake Oven, near Grand Tower, in southern Illinois:

"On those nights when the hill was flooded with gentle moonlight, visitors would report that they had seen a weird and mist-like creature…floating silently across their pathway to disappear among the rocks or in the dense bushes on the hillside. This disappearance was often followed by moans, wails and shrieks, such as only a ghost can make."*

These are the stories that we heard, shivering even on a hot night, before a fire at summer camp. But in the age of television and computer games I wonder: from where will the new camp stories come?

Perhaps we'll rely on the old favorites, such as werewolves or even vampires. After all, vampires were abroad in Illinois and the Midwest as recently as the 1980s. And if you don't believe me, you can ask the police of several neighboring states.

Feasting on the blood of others, even on human tissue, is unfortunately linked to Illinois. Before European settlement, the state's Woodland Indians practiced ceremonial cannibalism. Before them, so too did the mysterious mound-building residents of prehistoric Cahokia and Aztalan, but in a more casual way. Into their garbage heaps were tossed the refuse from dining tables: bones of birds, of fish, of small mammals and men—human bones scored by copper knives, split for their succulent marrow, to be unearthed 30 centuries later by men of science.

Cahokia's residents lived in the Midwest for 4,000 years, or so the anthropologists tell us. In their ancient wake they left the effigy

---

* Folklorist John W. Allen, quoted in Loren Coleman's *Mysterious America*.

mounds that dot shorelines. Did they invest the land with their spirit, and their spirit's hunger? Or was it something already bound into the earth, reaching to those who passed, and continue to pass, above?

Popular histories of vampirism trace the Dracula created by 19th-century novelist Bram Stoker back to Vlad Tepes, the bloodthirsty but not blood-sucking ruler of Wallachia, now Romania, in the 15th century. He was an especially cruel ruler but not the traditionally debonair figure of Hollywood. Real vampire legends go back further and are far darker.

In the 12th century William of Newburgh wrote about a man who was so evil that he would not stay dead. "For by the power of Satan in the dark hours, he was wont to come forth from his tomb and wander about all the streets, prowling round the houses, whilst on every side dogs were howling the whole night long." The monster was put to rest when two brothers opened his grave. The corpse was "gorged and swollen," its face "florid and chubby." Closer to our own time, in 1732, near Belgrade, a supposed vampire was exhumed and was discovered to possess fresh, ruddy skin and long nails. The mouth was "slobbered with blood from its last night's repast."

Can it be that some of us aspire to this evil, in the belief that the powers of the supernatural vampire may be inseparable from the creature's deeds?

Next door to Illinois, in November of 1996, police in Murray, Kentucky, arrested five too-real teenagers who had been in the habit of cutting each other's limbs and sucking the blood. They also drank the blood of small animals that they had killed. They called themselves a vampire clan. The clan was arrested for fatally bludgeoning the parents of one of its members. "They honestly believe they're vampires," said Murray police detective Mike Jump, quoted by the Associated Press.

Similarly, in 1981, in the quiet Wisconsin town of Mineral Point, police chased what they hoped was merely a man, a sick man. Residents had told of a cape-clad, white-faced man, 6 feet tall, who jumped from shadowed places. Eventually, the stories had become common enough that no one felt embarrassed when the police were finally approached.

Jon Pepper was on patrol on Monday, March 30, when he saw the figure dressed like Dracula, lurking behind some tombstones in the city's cemetery. Pepper approached the figure and asked what he was doing. The "vampire" stood up, about 6 feet, 5 inches. It said nothing but began to run. Pepper gave chase. The figure leapt a 4-foot-high barbed-wire fence and was gone.

The department stationed extra officers at the cemetery. Several more sightings were made, with no capture. The whole affair was complicated on April Fool's Day, two days after the police chase. Residents took advantage of the "fun" the publicity offered by dressing as vampires and roaming area bars.

The figure remains a mystery. Was it a real vampire? Or just a man?

"I've got enough other things going that I don't need to go around chasing vampires," said Mineral Point Police Lieutenant Bill Trott. "But if it is somebody with a problem, I'd like to catch him before he plays out his fantasy."

In Spring Valley, Illinois, 80 miles southwest of Chicago, there is a graveyard that has drawn those hoping to disbelieve. There are rumors of vampires, of dogs found dead there, drained of blood. In 1967 two teenagers broke into the crypt of three well-to-do bachelor butchers, the Massock brothers, and stole the head from one of the corpses. The teens were captured and punished, and an explanation for the cemetery's reputation seemed to have been delivered. But incidents continued.

According to Rosemary Ellen Guiley, in her book *The Complete Vampire Companion*, in the 1980s a Vietnam veteran and some friends went to the graveyard to see for themselves if the stories were true. They found a gaunt, pale figure that seemed to radiate evil. The veteran shot the figure at close range five times, with no effect. It approached them, and they ran.

A Chicago writer gathered a party and investigated, and turned to the crypt. They rapped on the crypt's door and received no response. They poked a stick into a small vent. A black and wormy something shot out from the hole and coiled up on the ground, whereupon they fled. They returned at dusk, with holy water, and emptied it into the hole.

To their astonishment, a "painful groaning" was heard from within.

If you would like to repeat the experiment, I would be interested in what you find out... but please don't ask me along.

* * *

If vampires are strange, then what about giant birds that steal children? On July 25, 1977, 10-year-old Marlan Lowe was playing with two other boys in his yard in Lawndale, a neighborhood in Chicago. Then they saw two gigantic birds diving toward them.

"I took off running, and all I know is I just felt something grabbing me by my shirt and picking me off the ground," recalled Lowe recently. "I just looked and up and here was this big old bird. I screamed. I was beating on this bird."

His mother, Ruth, heard his screams and came out. By now Lowe, who weighed 60 pounds, had been carried to the far corner of the house next door. She grabbed his dangling legs, and the bird dropped Lowe.

"I'll always remember how that huge thing was bending its white-ringed neck, and seemed to be trying to peck at Marlon, as it was flying away," Ruth Lowe said. The boy's brilliant red hair turned gray, and he wouldn't go outside at night.

Marlon Lowe's two birds surely were monsters, yet human monsters are always worse. After the incident, people started leaving dead birds on the Lowe family's porch, including an eagle.

The giant birds, or two like them, were captured on film five days later, 50 miles away, by a former military cameraman. He estimated the larger bird's wingspan to be between 18 and 20 feet, or twice as large as any bird known to exist today (one prehistoric bird weighed as much as 200 pounds and had a wingspan of as much as 25 feet). The film does not give any indication of the birds' size, but it does show a bird with wings like those of a buzzard or hawk, with a long, straight tail.

There is a long history of giant birds in Illinois, going back to the Native Americans' legends of the titanic Thunderbird, said to have been seen in the company of storms. Even today, birds of all kinds often flock just ahead of storm fronts, where they are buoyed by updrafts or "thermals." A gigantic bird would be dependant on such thermals to maintain flight.

More recently, in January 1948, 12-year-old James Trares of Glendale ran inside his house and told his mother, "There's a bird outside as big as a B-29!" The bird was gray-green and flying toward the sun. The boy said he knew it wasn't an aircraft because whatever it was, it flapped its wings.

On April 4, 1948, a farmer in Alton named Walter Siegmund also saw something strange in the air. "I thought there was something wrong with my eyesight," he said. "But it was definitely a bird and not a...plane. It appeared to be flying northeast. Two army planes had just flown over in the same direction, and I thought it was a pursuit craft following them. But from the movements of the object and its size, I figured it could only be a bird of tremendous size."

On April 9, 1949, Mrs. Robert Price of Caledonia saw "a monster bird, bigger than an airplane," with a long neck and powerful wings. Shortly thereafter, Veryl Babb of Freeport saw it, too, "but at first I didn't say anything because I thought people would laugh. When I read that Price had seen it, I decided to report it after all."

On the morning of the 10th the bird was seen at Overland by Clyde Smith. "I first saw it when I was out in the yard that morning," he said. "I thought it was a type of plane I had never seen before. It was circling and banking in a way I had never seen a plane perform, and I kept waiting for it to fall."

That afternoon Smith saw it again, as did his wife and Les Bacon. Like Siegmund, they at first thought it was a pursuit aircraft, but then it began to flap its wings. They said it was gray.

On April 24, E. M. Coleman, of Alton, and his 15-year-old son, James, spotted the giant bird. "It was an enormous, incredible thing with a body that looked like a naval torpedo," the father said. "It was flying at about 500 feet and cast a shadow the same size as that of a Piper Cub [airplane] at the same height."

That night, just across the Mississippi from Illinois, at St. Louis, police officers Clarence Johnson and Francis Hennelly saw the bird as it flew across the face of the moon. "The thing was as big as an airplane," said Hennelly. "Its wings were flapping and it was headed southwest, flying at an altitude of several hundred feet. I thought it was a large eagle, but I've never seen one that big before." Other St. Louis sightings followed.

Sometime in July 1977, James Major saw a giant bird west of Arlington. On the 27th so did Frank Jackson, in Lincoln. Stan Thompson observed it there a day later. On July 31 it was seen by Mrs. Albert Dunham, of Bloomington. On August 11 John Chappell saw it in Odin, and on July 30 it was seen in Downs.

Less threatening but just as mysterious was the Illinois crop circle discovered just west of Grayville, in rural Edwards County, not far from the border with White County. Most commonly found in England, crop circles seem to appear suddenly, usually at night. They range from simple circles of wheat that has fallen into overlapping and often braided whorls to complex chains of geometric shapes. The stalks are not broken but have been found in laboratories to have been subjected to

THE MAD GASSER OF MATTOON

On the morning of August 31, 1944, a man living in Mattoon, southwest of Decatur, got up from bed, stumbled to the bathroom, and threw up. He woke his wife and asked if she had left the gas on. She didn't think so, she said, but she'd check. But she couldn't move. She was paralyzed.

In another part of Mattoon, a woman woke up when she heard her daughter coughing. The mother tried to get up. She could hardly walk.

The next night, around 11, Mrs. Bert Kearney was asleep in her bedroom with her daughter, Dorothy, age three. Dorothy awoke to a strange smell.

"I first noticed a sickening sweet odor in the bedroom," the mother recalled. "But at the time I thought it might be from flowers outside the window. But the odor grew stronger and I began to feel a paralysis of my legs and lower body. I got frightened and screamed." She later experienced burned lips and a parched mouth and throat.

These were the first alleged acts of Mattoon's "Mad Gasser," a phantom or madman who for unknown reasons delighted in drugging residents with strange vapors. Or, as officials and the Journal of Abnormal and Social Psychology later claimed, it was all mass hysteria.

That opinion came only later. The yard of the Kearney family was immediately searched, as was the entire neighborhood, but no clues were found. At 12:30 the next day, though, Mr. Kearney returned from work. At one of his home's windows was a stranger who was "tall, dressed in dark clothing and wearing a tight-fitting cap." The figure immediately fled.

The gasser struck four more times by September 5. All the victims reported smelling the sickly sweet gas, after which they became nauseous and partially paralyzed for as long as an hour and a half. But on the 5th came the first physical evidence.

Carl and Beulah Cordes had come home through their back door, at about 10:30 p.m. Beulah went to the front of the house, to open the porch door, and just outside saw a white cloth. She picked it up and noticed it was damp. "When I inhaled the fumes from the cloth, I had a sensation similar to coming in contact with a strong electric current," she later said. "The feeling faced down my body to my feet and then seemed to settle in my knees. It was a feeling of paralysis."

She threw up. Her lips and face became swollen and inflamed. Her mouth began to bleed. She could not speak.

Two hours later she was fine, and on the porch police found an empty lipstick tube and a skeleton key. The same night, another woman had heard someone at her bedroom window and instantly found herself paralyzed by a gas.

Mattoon's police chief, E. C. Cole, ordered his officers to begin 24-hour duty. The city commissioner of public health asked for a state investigation. The cloth was sent to the University of Illinois; it yielded no clues.

The next night brought three attacks: Mrs. Ardell Spangler at 10, Mrs. Laura Junken shortly after midnight, and Fred Goble at 1 a.m. Goble's neighbor, Robert Daniels, said he'd seen a "tall man" fleeing the house. Friday brought news of attacks on Mrs. Cordie Taylor and on Glenda Hendershott, age 11.

Mayor E. E. Richardson announced that the city would post a reward for the gasser if he were not soon captured. One suspect was caught but later released after he passed a lie-detector test. The FBI was called in.

On Friday, Mrs. Violet Driskell and her daughter, Romona, 11, heard someone trying to remove the storm window from their bedroom window. They ran onto the porch to yell for help, but for Romona it was too late—already she was stumbling and nauseous. But Violet saw the figure as he ran away.

Just two hours and 45 minutes later, Mrs. Russell Bailey, Katherine Tuzzo, Genevieve Haskell, and a 7-year-old boy were sleeping in a common room. The window was partly open. Through it came a gas, and all were stricken. That same night, the principal of Columbian Grade School, Frances Smith, and her sister, Maxine, also were attacked. They first noticed an odor but soon saw a blue smoky vapor. At the same time, they believed, they heard a "buzzing sound," perhaps from the phantom's equipment.

The next night, police, farmers, and citizens patrolled Mattoon. There were at least six more attacks. Appealing for calm, the police commissioner stated, "There is no doubt but that a gas maniac exists and has made a number of attacks. But many of the reported attacks are nothing more than hysteria. Fear of the gas man is entirely out of proportion to the menace of the relatively harmless gas he is spraying."

Hardly reassuring, but the police agreed. Chief Cole announced, "We find absolutely no evidence to support stories that have been told. Hysteria must be blamed for such seemingly accurate accounts of supposed victims." He suggested that carbon tetrachloride drifting from the nearby Atlas Imperial Diesel Engine Company might be responsible. The company disagreed, pointing out that they used the chemical only for cleaning, and anyway it was odorless and produced no ill effects in the air.

Sunday Mr. and Mrs. Kenneth Fitzpatrick were gassed in their kitchen, as were three sisters. On the 13th, a "woman dressed in man's clothing" sprayed gas into the bedroom of Mrs. Bertha Bench. Footprints of high heels were found outside her window the next day.

In exploring the series of incidents for his 1983 book Mysterious America, author Loren Coleman found that witnesses stuck to their stories decades later. And he discovered that a few months before the Mattoon incidents, on February 1, three people in Coatesville, Pennsylvania, had reported a "sweet smelling gas" in their home, as did their neighbors. The three died, though the neighbors survived.

Was it all mass hysteria in Mattoon? Ironically, today the community is home to the Illinois Emergency Services Management Association, which is dedicated to bettering emergency management through education, planning, and improved response. Should the gasser ever return, his reception will not include hysteria.

sudden and intense heat, which can be duplicated, so far, only by microwave cooking. There have been a great many hoaxed circles, of course, many of them quite complex, which have broken, unbraided stalks. In England, the creation of such circles has become a sort of popular underground folk art, complicating serious research. There are many theories explaining the circles, and virtually no real evidence: they are symbols inscribed on the earth by rays from distant planets, as signs of intelligence, and can be translated into mathematical theorems; or they are created by UFOs, perhaps for the same reason, or as signposts; or they are signposts for travelers in time, using time machines that we call UFOs; or they are found perhaps naturally in sites having mystical and/or geomagnetic significance, and were important to the Druids, and give off strange effects best perceived by dowsers; or they are made not from the air but from inside the planet, by denizens of the hollow earth; or each and every one of them is a hoax.

Despite the last, there are accounts of simple crop circles as far back as the Middle Ages, though the descriptions of these are hardly indistinguishable from the simple "saucer nests" or merely flattened vegetation associated with alleged UFO landing sites of modern times.

Whatever it was, Illinois' crop circle appeared in a cornfield on October 12, 1996, and covered an acre. It was discovered by 82-year-old farmer Robert Hortin and his 27-year-old grandson, John. The circle was described as having a gigantic "horseshoe-shaped" swirl. The field was farmed by Gary Bunting and Donnie Perkins.

I'm a little suspicious of the circle, as another description of it included the detail that the stalks of corn had upturned roots, something not found in traditional British wheat-field circles. There, the shafts of the plants bend without breaking, and the plants are not uprooted. Still, corn is corn, not wheat, and I suppose we must make allowances.

It is known that hail can "paint" unusual geometric patterns. In an unspecified Illinois cornfield on June 29, 1976, according to the *American Meteorological Society Bulletin*, straight, distinct, parallel stripes of broken stalks were found following a hail storm. "The hail-stripes were easily located in the fields. They were measured and varied considerably in size. Most extended across the field and had widths of more than 15 to 25 meters."

And what about when it rained worms on Auburn, in January 1878? Or when it rained frogs on Cairo in August 1883? When it rained fish on Chicago, in June 1937, or when money rained in the city in December 1975? These sorts of things are called "falls" in the lexicon of unexplained phenomena. All sorts of things come down, such as spiderwebs on Evanston, in October 1922, and metal foil on Oak Park in November 1957. Scientists suggest the probable explanation of tornadoes and waterspouts sweeping up objects and transporting them many miles before they fall.

But the rain of hot cinders encountered in Ottawa, on June 17, 1857, is more likely associated with a meteor. The witness, writing to the *American Journal of Science,* said, "The cinders fell in a northwesterly direction in the shape of the letter 'V.' The weather had been showery, but I heard no thunder and saw no lightning. There appeared to be a small, dense black cloud hanging over the garden in a westerly direction, or a little to the south of west. The cinders fell upon a slight angle within about three rods of where I was at work; there was no wind at the moment, or none perceptible. My attention was first called to the freak the wind had in the grass, and the next moment to a hissing noise caused by the cinders passing through the air. The longer ones were considerably imbedded in the earth, so much as only to show a small part of it, while the smaller ones were about one-half buried. I noticed at the time that the ground where I afterwards picked up the cinders showed signs of warmth."

But how did Mrs. S. W. Culp come to find a gold chain embedded in a lump of coal in Morrisonville in 1891? How did a Roman coin come to be found in Cass County in 1882? And the other Roman coin found in Taylorville in 1883? What about the "moving tree stump" in Ridgway in 1976?

It is a fact that on Christmas Eve, 1885, Mrs. Patrick Rooney of Ottawa burst into flame for no reason at all and died of what can only be called spontaneous human combustion. Science does not yet recognize this phenomenon, but neither does it offer any theory to explain how people throughout history have suddenly been consumed by intense fire from within, having only the most minimal effect on their surroundings. Mrs. Rooney weighed 200 pounds, but her remains consisted of only a burned piece of skull, two charred vertebrae, a foot, and a small pile of ashes. They were found at the bottom of a 3-by-4-foot hole burned in the floor. Her sleeping husband died of asphyxiation, from her smoke.

These happenings, these tragedies, these brushes with other realms—these must not be forgotten, if only to honor the intellectual curiosity and emotional resilience of our forbears. I've covered only the broadest categories of the bizarre and unnatural. There are lots more mysteries out there, hidden in your local historical societies and in the memories of your oldest neighbors.

Go and find them. Let me know. And tell the stories at camp.

INDEX

(Unless otherwise indicated,
municipal and county place names are in Illinois.)

MORE GREAT TITLES

The W-Files: True Reports of Wisconsin's Unexplained Phenomena
Jay Rath

The M-Files: True Reports of Minnesota's Unexplained Phenomena
Jay Rath

Foods That Made Wisconsin Famous
Richard J. Baumann

Great Minnesota Walks: 49 Strolls, Rambles, Hikes, and Treks
Wm. Chad McGrath

Creating a Perennial Garden in the Midwest
Joan Severa

The Spirit of Door County: A Photographic Essay
Darryl R. Beers

Up North Wisconsin: A Region for All Seasons
Sharyn Alden

Great Wisconsin Taverns: 101 Distinctive Badger Bars
Dennis Boyer

Great Wisconsin Restaurants
Dennis Getto

Great Wisconsin Walks: 45 Strolls, Rambles, Hikes, and Treks
Wm. Chad McGrath

Great Weekend Adventures
the Editors of Wisconsin Trails

Best Canoe Trails of Southern Wisconsin
Michael E. Duncanson

County Parks of Wisconsin: 600 Parks You Can Visit Featuring 25 Favorites
Jeannette and Chet Bell

The Wisconsin Traveler's Companion: A Guide to Country Sights
Jerry Apps and Julie Sutter-Blair

W Is for Wisconsin
Dori Hillestad Butler and Eileen Dawson

Walking Tours of Wisconsin's Historic Towns
Lucy Rhodes, Elizabeth McBride, and Anita Matcha

Best Wisconsin Bike Trips
Phil Van Valkenberg

Wisconsin: The Story of the Badger State
Norman K. Risjord

Paddling Northern Wisconsin
Mike Svob

Barns of Wisconsin
Jerry Apps

Portrait of the Past: A Photographic Journey Through Wisconsin 1865–1920
Howard Mead, Jill Dean, and Susan Smith

TRAILS BOOKS
P.O. Box 5650, Madison, WI 53705
(800) 236-8088
e-mail: info@wistrails.com
www.wistrails.com